AF254466

DESTINY

And The Three Battles You Must Win to Get There

GARY KEESEE

Published by Free Indeed Publishing.
Distributed by Faith Life Now.
Faith Life Now
P.O. Box 779
New Albany, OH 43054
1-(888)-391-LIFE
You can reach Faith Life Now on the Internet at www.faithlifenow.com.

TABLE OF CONTENTS

INTRODUCTION

Destiny. The word brings with it a wonder and a confidence. It infers a future that was planned outside of your own decision. To most people, it speaks of a place of great happiness and fulfillment. But if there is a place called destiny, do we arrive there automatically, or do we have a part to play in finding it? Do people have a destiny that has been planned by God before they were born? In my book, *Destiny: And the Three Battles You Must Win to Get There*, we will find that God does indeed have a destiny for every believer. I am not talking about heaven, which of course every believer inherits when they come to Christ. No, I am talking about purpose and assignment while on the earth.

We will look at some famous biblical characters and watch how God brought about their destiny and what they had to do to step into God's plan. I will also cover much of my story and how God brought my family out of desperate poverty where we lived for nine years, to now hosting a TV program called, *Fixing the Money Thing* which reaches a potential audience of seven billion people daily. I'll share how we broke the debt cycle and started a multimillion-dollar company that has helped hundreds of thousands escape the slavery of debt.

As the author of over twenty books on the subject of financial freedom, and discovering the good life that God has for you, I trust this book will help you not only discover your God-given destiny but will encourage you to fight for it.

> *I press on toward the goal to win the prize for which God has called me heavenward in Christ Jesus.*
>
> —Philippians 3:14 (NIV)

—Gary Keesee

CHAPTER ONE

THE MYSTERY OF DESTINY

When we are born, we do not know much. But hidden in God's plan for us, and hidden from us, is greatness. God cannot reveal our created purpose in full disclosure at this stage of our life, not because He does not love us, but because He does love us. He knows we are much too young to understand His plan at that point. And, basically, we do not need to know His plan yet. The training of our character and learning obedience must qualify us for that revelation. Until then, we walk a somewhat normal existence. But even during those early years, as we are learning and growing, there are major clues to our future. Our hobbies and interests, what we like to do in our spare time, and how we handle life in general all show us clues to our future.

I have five children, and they are all completely different from each other with different personalities, different temperaments, and interests. Some of them are extremely detailed, wanting everything in its place. Others are creative and couldn't care less if their bedroom is clean or not. We do not think much about those differences when we are young. We just realize we like certain things and some things not so much. But those interests draw us toward our future. They will affect future decisions and set our course toward our destiny.

If you had asked me when I was in high school if I had ever thought about pastoring a church or doing a daily TV broadcast, I would have laughed in your face. But today I am a pastor and have pastored for over 30 years. And yes, I do a daily TV broadcast, called *Fixing the Money Thing*, which currently can reach 7 billion people on a daily basis. I own a multimillion-dollar financial services corporation that operates in all 50 states, helping people get out of debt and safeguard their investments. That company has helped thousands over the years and has produced millions of dollars in profits, which have funded our outreach to the nations. Did I know this was going to happen? No, not at all. So then, you should ask, how did that happen? Well, I wish I could say it is because of how great I am, or that I possess such great knowledge, I couldn't help it. WRONG! Write this down:

ONLY GOD KNOWS WHAT AND WHERE YOUR DESTINY IS!

Let's say you saw a screwdriver for the first time in your life. If you did not know anything about screws, you would have no idea what it does or why it was created. But the one who created the screwdriver would know exactly what it was designed to do. Only the one who created you could tell you why He created you the way He did. But I can guarantee you this, you are unique!!!! You are designed for a very special purpose.

Satan does not want you to find out just how unique you are. He uses people to mock your uniqueness. We all want to fit in, letting culture dictate what we wear and what we do. But it is your uniqueness that makes you so valuable. Speaking of screwdrivers, have you ever seen those really big screwdrivers that are designed to turn really big screws? They work fine when you are working on a big piece of equipment, but when you are working on your wristwatch, those big heavy screwdrivers would crush the watch. Instead, they make really tiny screwdrivers to work on delicate watches. Before you make fun of the tiny screwdriver, realize that there may be a day when you will need that tiny screwdriver. And on that day, the design and purpose of that tiny screwdriver will become crystal clear, and you will celebrate its unique design and functionality.

You are not like anyone else! No one else has the same fingerprints you have, no one has the same retina scan you have, and no one has the same DNA you have. These are three methods that we use today to confirm your unique identity. Those kinds of unique differences are all throughout your creation. But those are just surface-level differences. It is a fact; there is no one like you. Are these differences just by chance, or did God actually create you with these differences for a reason? Let's look at a few Bible characters and see if we can see God's hand on them at a young age, for an assignment that they knew nothing about.

> *Before I formed you in the womb I knew you, before you were born, I set you apart; I appointed you as a prophet to the nations.*
>
> —Jeremiah 1:5 (NIV)

This is an incredible revelation from our Creator. Before God even formed Jeremiah, He knew exactly what he was destined to do. He was actually appointed and called as a prophet to the nations before he was even formed. God knew the purpose He had for Jeremiah before he was formed and made him specifically for that purpose. He created him with the talents and giftings he would need for his unique assignment.

What about Moses? Born in obscurity, hidden illegally, Moses's life was not an ordinary journey! In the first chapter of Exodus, a new Pharaoh came to power who did not know Joseph, the history of the famine, and the plan that Joseph put in place to save Egypt years ago. Alarmed by the exploding population of the Hebrews, he ordered all the male babies to be killed when they were born. But the midwives ignored his order, saying that the Hebrew women were much stronger than the Egyptian women and gave birth before the midwives could get to them. Then, Pharaoh gave the order that every Hebrew baby boy born must be thrown into the Nile River.

> *Now a man of the tribe of Levi married a Levite woman, and she became pregnant and gave birth to a son. When she saw that he was a fine child, she hid him for three months. But when she could hide him no longer, she got a papyrus basket for him and coated it with tar and pitch. Then she placed the child in it and put it among the reeds along the bank of the Nile.*
>
> —Exodus 2:1–3 (NIV)

> *Then Pharaoh's daughter went down to the Nile to bathe, and her attendants were walking along the riverbank. She saw the basket among the reeds and sent her female slave to get it. She opened it and saw the baby. He was crying, and she felt sorry for him. "This is one of the Hebrew babies," she said.*

> *Then his sister asked Pharaoh's daughter, "Shall I go and get one of the Hebrew women to nurse the baby for you?"*

> *"Yes, go," she answered. So the girl went and got the baby's mother. Pharaoh's daughter said to her, "Take this baby and nurse him for me, and I will pay you." So the woman took the baby and nursed him. When the child grew older, she took him to Pharaoh's*

daughter and he became her son. She named him Moses, saying, "I drew him out of the water."

—Exodus 2:5–10 (NIV)

What were the chances that Pharaoh's daughter would find the baby and decide to keep it? This was God's plan, part of the puzzle of his destiny. Moses's destiny required him to know all about the Egyptian culture and language. He needed to know the laws and protocol of the palace. Did Moses himself plan this? No, God did, before he was even born. Moses was raised as a leader in the most powerful government of his time. He would need the skills he learned being raised within the Egyptian political system later on, when he would lead over 2 million Hebrews out of slavery. Of course, at this early stage of his life, he did not know that, but God did.

Moses was educated in all the wisdom of the Egyptians and was powerful in speech and action.

—Acts 7:22 (NIV)

He understood the Egyptian culture completely; he knew how the government worked and was well acquainted with the royal family and the palace functions. He also spoke fluent Egyptian, which comes in handy when you are standing before Pharaoh. And, no, he did not stutter!

What about your brother, Aaron the Levite? I know he can speak well. He is already on his way to meet you, *and he will be glad to see you. You shall speak to him and put words in his mouth; I will help both of you speak and will teach you what to do. **He will speak to the people for you.***

—Exodus 4:14-16 (NIV)

The issue was that Moses was raised as an Egyptian and did not speak the language of the Hebrews well, not that he stuttered.

What about Joseph? At the age of seventeen, he had two dreams that prophesied he would one day be a ruler, and his family would bow down to him. But at the time, he was just a shepherd. How would that ever happen? I think you might know the story. His brothers were jealous of him and sold him to some traders who traveled through their area. Those traders took him into Egypt and sold him as a slave to Potiphar.

Now Joseph had been taken down to Egypt. Potiphar, an Egyptian who was one of Pharaoh's officials, the captain of the guard, bought him from the Ishmaelites who had taken him there.

The Lord was with Joseph so that he prospered, and he lived in the house of his Egyptian master. When his master saw that the Lord was with him and that the Lord gave him success in everything he did, Joseph found favor in his eyes and became his attendant.

> *Potiphar put him in charge of his household, and he entrusted to his care everything he owned.*
>
> —Genesis 39:1–4 (NIV)

Here we see the same thing, a purposed plan that was laid out before Joseph was born. His destiny required him to be raised, as Moses was, with a complete understanding of the Egyptian laws and government systems, to know the language and how to relate to the Egyptian culture. Look at verse four again, "Potiphar put him in charge of his household, and he entrusted to his care everything he owned." If Potiphar put him in charge of his entire household and put him in charge of everything he owned, Joseph had to have learned everything there was to know about living in Egypt. But his journey does not end there. Potiphar's house was not his destiny; it was simply training for his destiny!

It just so happened that Potiphar was the captain of the palace guard. This gave Joseph an inside understanding of how things worked in the palace, as well as information and training he could not have gotten anywhere else. I am sure, as the one who ran Potiphar's entire estate, that Joseph rubbed elbows with some of Egypt's highest officials as well as officials who came from other nations. But this was not where he was destined to stay. This was part of the required training he needed to occupy the destiny that God had for him later.

He was later falsely accused of adultery with Potiphar's wife and thrown in prison. During that time, two former employees of Pharaoh were thrown into prison with him. Both of these former employees had dreams they could not understand. They asked Joseph if he had any idea what the dreams meant, and Joseph asked God to give him the interpretation for them. What Joseph said the dreams meant is exactly what happened. Later, one of the employees returned to work for Pharaoh's court, and when Pharaoh himself had a dream he could not understand, this employee mentioned Joseph to him.

> *So Pharaoh sent for Joseph, and he was quickly brought from the dungeon. When he had shaved and changed his clothes, he came before Pharaoh.*
>
> *Pharaoh said to Joseph, "I had a dream, and no one can interpret it. But I have heard it said of you that when you hear a dream you can interpret it."*
>
> *"I cannot do it," Joseph replied to Pharaoh, "but God will give Pharaoh the answer he desires."*
>
> —Genesis 41:14–16 (NIV)

Joseph successfully interpreted the dreams for Pharaoh. He then gave Pharoah an administrative plan to prepare for the famine that was to come after seven years of very great harvests.

> *God has shown Pharaoh what he is about to do. Seven*

years of great abundance are coming throughout the land of Egypt, but seven years of famine will follow them. Then all the abundance in Egypt will be forgotten, and the famine will ravage the land. The abundance in the land will not be remembered, because the famine that follows it will be so severe. The reason the dream was given to Pharaoh in two forms is that the matter has been firmly decided by God, and God will do it soon.

"And now let Pharaoh look for a discerning and wise man and put him in charge of the land of Egypt. Let Pharaoh appoint commissioners over the land to take a fifth of the harvest of Egypt during the seven years of abundance. They should collect all the food of these good years that are coming and store up the grain under the authority of Pharaoh, to be kept in the cities for food. This food should be held in reserve for the country, to be used during the seven years of famine that will come upon Egypt, so that the country may not be ruined by the famine."

The plan seemed good to Pharaoh and to all his officials. So Pharaoh asked them, "Can we find anyone like this man, one in whom is the spirit of God?" Then Pharaoh said to Joseph, "Since God has made all this known to you, there is no one so discerning and wise as you. You shall be in charge of my palace, and all my people are to submit to your orders. Only with

respect to the throne will I be greater than you."
—Genesis 41:28–40 (NIV)

It should be noted that it was not having the correct interpretation of the dream Pharaoh had that prompted him to put Joseph in charge. That was just to give him credibility. It was Joseph's detailed plan on how to prepare and survive the coming seven-year famine that impressed Pharaoh. This was Joseph's destiny: to rule over Egypt and to bring his family from Canaan to live there with him during the horrible years of famine. The dreams he had as a teenager, which made no sense to him or his family, came to pass just as God had shown him. It is obvious that this was God's plan for him before he was created in his mother's womb!

Of course, we can all agree that Jesus was put in Mary's womb by the Holy Spirit expressly for the mission that Jesus carried out. Do you see a pattern here?

The stories I just mentioned are all very powerful examples of God's plan for people's lives. But what about you and me, just ordinary people? Does God have an exact destiny planned for us? Maybe we are not just ordinary people. Maybe we are special and uniquely crafted by God Himself.

I praise you because I am fearfully and wonderfully made; your works are wonderful, I know that full well.
—Psalm 139:14 (NIV)

As detailed as nature is, I believe that all that God creates is detailed and designed. So, YES! I believe that God has a destiny and a unique purpose for every person created. Take, for instance, the 2026 Super Bowl between the Seahawks and the Patriots. Following the Seattle Seahawks' victory, head coach Mike Macdonald expressed that he believes God called him to be a coach, stating, "I believe God called me to be a coach, and I listened to Him." He shared this sentiment after winning the Super Bowl championship in his second season as the head coach. Macdonald, 38, led the Seahawks to the championship, becoming one of the youngest coaches to achieve this. I do not know his history, but I bet if you looked back at his life, you could see the path that led him to that one moment.

He was literally preparing for that moment years before his Super Bowl win. But why football? Why not soccer or car racing? Because God put a passion for football in him. As the winning champion, he stood in front of 200 million people and declared his faith in God to all who would listen. Now every young boy or girl who loves sports is being inspired to follow after God as well. I am sure his influence will continue for years ahead. What about you? Do you have a destiny, a place that God has already designed you to occupy? I believe you do, but I also know, like in all the cases I just mentioned, there is a journey required to get there.

I call the beginning part of our journey toward destiny, "the season of preparation." This is the longest part of our journey, usually taking years. Through this season, the future is not plain; it is still hidden. But know that God knows exactly where you are and He knows your name.

God knew where Moses was when He spoke to him out of a burning bush. God knew where Joseph was when he was in the Egyptian prison with a life sentence. God knew where David was as he watched over his sheep. And God knows where you are.

When I started doing TV, I was really scared. I didn't know anything about TV or how to pay for it. But God has a way of encouraging us on our journey just when we think we cannot go on. On one particular day, my secretary called, all excited. She said that she had just gotten off the phone with someone who called in asking to buy one of every product we had. My secretary, Tracy, was a little surprised by this, and the lady on the phone could tell. So, she told Tracy why she was buying all these products. She said that she and her husband were in bad shape financially, and were so discouraged. But in the night, she had a dream where this guy named Gary Keesee was talking about getting out of debt.

She woke her husband up and asked him if he knew anyone named Gary Keesee, as she had no idea who I was. Her husband said he had no idea who I was, either. She was a little confused. The next morning, she turned on the TV, and there I was, teaching on how to be debt-free. She was

I AM TELLING YOU, GOD KNOWS YOUR NAME! HE KNOWS MUCH MORE THAN THAT; HE KNOWS WHAT HE HAS CREATED YOU TO DO AND TO BE.

shocked and so excited. So, she picked up the phone, called our office, and ordered all of our products to learn how to get out of debt. Her story inspired me, and I was so encouraged by it. God knows my name! If He knows my name, then He knows about everything else that is going on, the money we need, the staff we need, everything! I was so encouraged that our TV broadcast was making a difference!

I am telling you, God knows your name! He knows much more than that. He knows what He has created you to do and to be.

So, be encouraged. You are extremely valuable to God.

CHAPTER TWO

YOU ARE UNIQUE AND DIFFERENT

I was walking down the Avenue des Champs-Élysées in Paris a few years ago, the famous shopping street with all the fashion windows. The color that year, according to the fashion I saw in the store windows, was either grey or black. Strange, I thought, as I enjoy seeing a splash of color in life. Certainly, black and grey cannot be everyone's favorite colors. But as I looked down the street, I saw thousands of shoppers that day, and not one of them had any color on. Everyone, and I mean everyone, was wearing either black or grey. I stood there amazed.

Was there not one person among the thousands there who wanted to wear something with color? Why is it so important that none of us stand out? Why do we want to blend into the crowd when God made us all so unique? Why do we dare not appear out of step with the norm of the day? Well, in reality, the norm is changing so fast you cannot keep up with it.

I was looking at an old picture from 1914 the other day. All the ladies had these really big hats on and all the men had their dress hats on. If you went back to that time period, those hats would have been completely normal and you probably would not want to be seen in public without yours.

Even now, my wife will say that she has nothing to wear while I look at her closet and wonder in amazement at what she just said. Upon further investigation, I find that she admits that she has clothes but not new ones, and the ones she has are all the wrong color. The wrong color? I will have to admit, I really do not keep up with fashion, that is Drenda's department. I am the guy who, every once in a while, hears, "You are not really going to wear that are you?" "No, of course not, I was just trying it on to be sure it will still fit twenty years from now when this fashion comes back around." One day, my wife got a little upset when she saw I was wearing two patterns that did not match. I was tempted to say, "Well, someone has to be the first one to change the style, but sadly it will not be me."

In reality, our uniqueness is our value. We are all created differently for a reason. Paul spoke a lot about this very topic in the book of First Corinthians. Paul knew he needed to address this area, or this young church was going to miss what God had for them, and even worse, they might miss God's plan for their lives completely. They were arguing about who was the greatest, who was more spiritual, and were trying to be seen for all the wrong reasons. Divisions

YOU WERE ALREADY CREATED AS AN EYE!

in the church were tearing the church apart, and unless Paul could straighten it out, the church itself might fall apart. So, he spent a lot of time covering the topic of identity and how God has made each of us unique. He emphasized that we each have our role in the body of Christ, and we all need each other.

Just as a body, though one, has many parts, but all its many parts form one body, so it is with Christ. For we were all baptized by one Spirit so as to form one body—whether Jews or Gentiles, slave or free—and we were all given the one Spirit to drink. Even so the body is not made up of one part but of many.

Now if the foot should say, "Because I am not a hand, I do not belong to the body," it would not for that reason stop being part of the body. And if the ear should say, "Because I am not an eye, I do not belong to the body," it would not for that reason stop being part of the body. If the whole body were an eye, where would the sense of hearing be? If the whole body were an ear, where would the sense of smell be? But in fact God has placed the parts in the body, every one of them, just as he wanted them to be. If they were all one part, where would the body be? As it is, there are many parts, but one body. The eye cannot say to the hand, "I don't need you!" And the head cannot say to the feet, "I don't need you!"

—1 Corinthians 12:12–21 (NIV)

Wow, isn't this just how culture is? Everyone is looking at Facebook, staring at all the photoshopped photos and wanting to be someone else instead of who they are.

Let's read this again, *"But in fact God has placed the parts in the body, every one of them,**_just as he wanted them to be_**"* (1 Corinthians 12:18, NIV). Let me paraphrase what God is saying: God has a purpose for the way He made you. Even if you want to be someone else, you will always be who He has created you to be. An eye can't say, "I want to be a foot," because it has already been created as an eye! You are an eye! And yes, God decided that before you were born.

You were already created as an eye! Besides creating you with absolutely unique qualities and characteristics, He placed you right where He wanted you in regard to the time you were born and where you were born!

> *From one man he made all the nations, that they (man) should inhabit the whole earth; and he marked out their appointed times in history and the **boundaries** of their lands.*
>
> —Acts 17:26 (NIV)

Paul speaks with a bit of frustration, in my opinion, about

how important it was for this church to stop looking at each other and instead start looking to God for their identity and value. I am going to put all fifteen verses here from his conversation with them concerning this, a rather long quote, but it is imperative that we all know this.

Brothers and sisters, I could not address you as people who live by the Spirit but as people who are still worldly—mere infants in Christ. I gave you milk, not solid food, for you were not yet ready for it. Indeed, you are still not ready. You are still worldly. For since there is jealousy and quarreling among you, are you not worldly? Are you not acting like mere humans? For when one says, "I follow Paul," and another, "I follow Apollos," are you not mere human beings?

What, after all, is Apollos? And what is Paul? Only servants, through whom you came to believe—as the Lord has assigned to each his task. I planted the seed, Apollos watered it, but God has been making it grow. So neither the one who plants nor the one who waters is anything, but only God, who makes things grow. The one who plants and the one who waters have one purpose, and they will each be rewarded according to their own labor. For we are co-workers in God's service; you are God's field, God's building.

By the grace God has given me, I laid a foundation as a wise builder, and someone else is building on it. But each one should build with care. For no one can lay any foundation other than the one already laid, which is Jesus Christ. If anyone builds on this foundation using gold, silver, costly stones, wood, hay or straw, their work will be shown for what it is, because the Day will bring it to light. It will be revealed with fire, and the fire will test the quality of each person's work. If what has been built survives, the builder will receive a reward. If it is burned up, the builder will suffer loss but yet will be saved—even though only as one escaping through the flames.

—1 Corinthians 3:1–15 (NIV)

Take a look at verse five again:

Only servants, as the Lord has assigned to each his task.

—1 Corinthians 3:5 (NIV)

And verse eight:

*The one who plants and the one who waters have **one purpose,** and they will each **be rewarded according to their own labor.***

—1 Corinthians 3:8 (NIV)

Then finally, verses 13 and 14:

Their work will be shown for what it is, because the

*Day will bring it to light. It will be revealed with fire, and the fire will test **the quality of each person's work.** If what has been built survives, the builder will receive a reward.*

—1 Corinthians 3:13–14 (NIV)

We are going to be judged on the quality of our work. What work? Any work we decide to do? **No, the work that has been assigned to us.** Paul is saying that if you build on what God has given you to do, it is like building with gold, silver, and costly stones. But if you build with straw, it doesn't cost you much and it shows you really do not care to follow God's directions. Yes, you did build something, but not what God wanted you to build.

Paul brings even more light to the subject in verse 10.

*By the **grace God has given me**, I laid a foundation as a wise builder.*

—1 Corinthians 3:10 (NIV)

Some versions say, "as an expert builder." Notice that Paul is saying that he had grace to be an expert builder. What kind of builder? He was an expert in laying the foundation. We know that Paul was an apostle, and he started churches all across Asia, laying their foundation on the revelation of Jesus Christ. God gave him the grace and ability to do that. But we know he did not have the grace to do everything. He admits that Apollos watered what he had planted, meaning he helped it grow. Paul stayed in his lane—you may have heard people use that phrase, "stay in your lane." Paul was focused. He continually spoke of a person's assignment to be like a race.

SO MANY PEOPLE ARE LIVING OUTSIDE OF THEIR GIFTING!

However, I consider my life worth nothing to me; my only aim is to finish the race and complete the task the Lord Jesus has given me—the task of testifying to the good news of God's grace.
—Acts 20:24 (NIV)

Paul speaks of taking aim and finishing his race, the one Jesus gave him to run. We all have our race to run, a purpose that God has for us. A race has a start and finish line, as well as boundaries to run in.

Do you not know that in a race all the runners run, but only one gets the prize? Run in such a way as to get the prize. Everyone who competes in the games goes into strict training. They do it to get a crown that will not last, but we do it to get a crown that will last forever. Therefore I do not run like someone running aimlessly; I do not fight like a boxer beating the air. No, I strike a blow to my body and make it my slave so that after I have preached to others, I myself will not be disqualified for the prize.
—1 Corinthians 9:24–27 (NIV)

You have grace also, but not for everything. God has given you a specific grace to accomplish what he has planned for you to do, which he designed for your life before you were born.

It amazes me how people love to do what they do. Take my dentist, for example. He spends all day in people's mouths doing such detailed work while bent over and working in such a small space. I would not want to do that! I have a friend who is a surgeon, and he loves it! He tells me how they put people back together with sutures, screws, and bolts. I have another friend who is a brain surgeon and has done thousands of brain surgeries. Again, I have no interest. Besides having no interest, I cannot even imagine doing it.

I also know people who love administration (praise God). I can work on administration for a little bit, and then it seems my brain starts to shut down. But I can teach on the Kingdom of God all day and come out just as excited as I started. Why? Because I am in my lane, I am staying in my strength, and instead of wearing me out, it empowers me.

So many people are living outside of their gifting! People working just for a paycheck, dreading Monday morning, and just enduring the week. We were not designed this way.

We were designed to live from passion and vision with an unlimited potential. But vision, passion, and an unlimited potential are hardly how most of the population lives. Here is the sad state of life from a few recent surveys.

Seventy-six precent of people in the US are living month to month, according to an article from civicscience.com.[1]

Fourty-four percent of households actually have <u>$250 or less</u> in discretionary income monthly after the bills are paid.[2]

---

1 "Living Paycheck to Paycheck in an Era of Financial Distress and 'Survival-Mode' Mentality," *Civic Science* online, January 20, 2026, https://civicscience.com/living-paycheck-to-paycheck-in-an-era-of-financial-distress-and-survival-mode-mentality.

2 Hiranmayi Srinivasan, "Nearly Half of Women Say They Have Less Than $250 Left Each Month After Paying Bills," *Investopedia* online, May 14, 2024, https://www.investopedia.com/nearly-half-of-women-say-they-have-less-than-usd250-left-each-month-after-paying-bills-8647057

Bankrate's annual study found in 2025 that 59% of Americans don't have enough savings to cover an unexpected $1,000 emergency,[3] and 37% could not pay a bill of $400.[4] That is **137 million people!!!!!!**

Besides not doing well financially, studies show that only about 21% of employees are actively satisfied, up to 79% feel disconnected or unmotivated, and are not engaged in what they do.[5]

So many people are surviving life instead of being led by vision and passion. Of course, this all goes back to the fall of man. Adam was created with a very definitive purpose and identity when he was placed on the earth.

> *"What is mankind that you are mindful of them, a son of man that you care for him? You made them a little lower than the angels; you crowned them with glory and honor and put everything under their feet." In putting everything under them, God left nothing that is not subject to them.*
>
> —Hebrews 2:6b–8a (NIV)

Adam was created to rule over the earth. In fact, there is nothing here that was not placed under his legal jurisdiction, and he was crowned with glory and honor. If you think of a

---

3 *Americans Backtrack: Just 41% Say They Could Pay A $1,000 Emergency Expense From Their Savings*, Bankrate, January 23, 2025. chrome-extension://efaidnbmnnnibpcajpcglclefindmkaj/https://www.bankrate.com/f/102997/x/1c62ee6b93/january-fsp-press-release-final.pdf

4 Aaron McDade, "Here's How Many Americans Can't Afford a $400 Emergency—The Numbers May Shock You," *Investopedia* online, September 22, 2025, https://www.investopedia.com/here-s-how-many-americans-can-t-afford-a-usd400-emergency-the-numbers-may-shock-you-11814788

5 "Global Data Summary—State of the Global Workplace 2025," *Gallup* online, https://www.gallup.com/workplace/697904/state-of-the-global-workplace-global-data.aspx?

king, he is crowned to be king. Although we crown a king, he is still the man he was before he was crowned. The change is that once crowned, he carries the authority of the government that crowned him. Once crowned, that government backs up every word he says. Adam ruled the earth on behalf of the Kingdom of God with that kind of authority. He occupied that place of honor and authority until he was deceived into believing Satan's lies and willfully committed treason against God. If we go to Genesis chapter three, we will see the result of that decision.

> *To Adam he said, "Because you listened to your wife and ate fruit from the tree about which I commanded you, 'You must not eat from it,' "Cursed is the ground because of you;* **through painful toil** *you will eat food from it all the days of your life. It will produce thorns and thistles for you, and you will eat the plants of the field.* **By the sweat of your brow** *you will eat your food until you return to the ground, since from it you were taken; for dust you are and to dust you will return."*
>
> —Genesis 3:17–19 (NIV)

Adam lost his position, and after being kicked out of the Garden of Eden, he lost his provision. He was left to survive on his own efforts as he had kicked God out of his life. Now, through his own painful toil and sweat, he would survive. I call this "the earth curse system." Adam was no longer motivated by passion but by survival. His assignment, which was to take care of the garden of God, was now replaced with painful toil and sweat just to survive. By the way, that earth curse system is still in place today. And like Adam, people have really lost sight of purpose and would love to find it, but survival gets in the way.

YOU WERE UNIQUELY CREATED WITH A PURPOSE, A DESTINY, A PLACE WHERE YOUR UNIQUE TALENTS AND PASSION WILL SHINE FORTH THE GLORY OF GOD IN A DARK WORLD.

If you consider that 76% of the population lives hand to mouth,[6] what kind of dreams are they going to have? I can tell you, they look for an escape from the pain, they look for rest on the weekend, vacations, or retirement. But how many really look forward to Monday? When was the last time you heard someone say, "I have to go to work"? You probably hear it a lot. When was the last time you heard someone say, "I get to go to work on Monday"?

People are living in debt, in a life of slavery! Passion? They do not have the luxury of working with passion. They need the money, so they take the job. They really do not have a clue who they are or what they have been created to do. They take jobs because of the pay, not because of passion. Everyone wants to become a millionaire, believing that having enough money will free them from the endless grindstone of painful toil and sweat. The good news is that Jesus paid the price to bring us back into the Kingdom of God as sons and daughters of God, where we can find provision and discover our purpose.

Consequently, you are no longer foreigners and strangers, but fellow citizens with God's people and also members of his household.

—Ephesians 2:19 (NIV)

6 "Living Paycheck to Paycheck in an Era of Financial Distress and 'Survival-Mode' Mentality," *Civic Science* online, January 20, 2026, https://civicscience.com/living-paycheck-to-paycheck-in-an-era-of-financial-distress-and-survival-mode-mentality/

Now, through our position in the Kingdom of God, we can prosper above the earth curse system. Through the leading of the Holy Spirit, we can walk free from the slavery of debt and meaningless labor. (For more information on living financially free, check out my five-book series, *Your Financial Revolution* at *garykeesee.com*).

So, in review, you were never created to be just like everyone else! In fact, I read an interesting stat the other day: the chances that someone could have your exact DNA sequence, outside of being an identical twin, are one in 70 trillion.[7] You were uniquely created with a purpose, a destiny, a place where your unique talents and passion will shine forth the glory of God in a dark world.

GOD CREATED YOU TO BE SOMEONE'S ANSWER, AND YOUR RESPONSE WILL POINT THEM TO JESUS.

When we talk like this, people begin to think that only a glamorous position like a movie star or rock star would qualify for destiny. But do you remember the dentist I mentioned, who is working in people's mouths every day? Although I said I would not want to do it, they love it!!!! They are motivated to do it. It is their passion. Their destiny is to serve people and God by being a dentist. Trust me, I had an infected tooth that hurt so bad that I would have paid any amount of money to have a dentist fix it. God calls people to do all kinds of things and leads people into every career path you can imagine. He wants His glory to be seen throughout the culture.

---

7 Sam Shead, "Can two people have the same DNA?" *BBC* online, https://www.sciencefocus.com/the-human-body/can-two-people-have-the-same-dna

I read an interesting story recently. In December of 2025, a semi-truck hauling bricks lost control on a snowy highway, crashing through a barrier and leaving the cab dangling about 100 feet above the ground from the top of a bridge. It was a life-threatening situation as the truck was unstable on the slippery road and could still slide off. It just so happened that a heavy-duty crane/wrecker, specifically suited for this type of recovery, and extremely rare to be in the area, happened to be nearby. The driver was stuck in the cab for over five hours. The heavy-duty machine was used to hold the truck in place as a firefighter was lowered to the cab to get the driver out.[8]

I heard through another report that there were only two of those heavy-duty machines in the state at the time and it just so happened that one of them was right there. Here is my point: we may think that the man who operates that machine is just a normal guy, nothing fancy, just another worker operating heavy equipment. But what if God created him with a desire to handle those big pieces of machinery, knowing that his expert skill-set would be needed in life to help people get things done, and in this case, save someone's life? How important was that man at that moment? The prophet Isaiah prophesied about the coming age of the church and addressed God's desire to lead people in all kinds of occupations.

They will be called oaks of righteousness, a planting of the Lord for the display of his splendor.

—Isaiah 61:3b (NIV)

---

8 Kieran Sullivan, Raymond Sanchez, "Must-watch: Truck driver rescued dangling off West Virginia highway 100-feet above the ground below" *Fox Weather* online, December 2, 2025, https://www.foxweather.com/extreme-weather/semi-truck-driver-rescued-after-dangling-from-west-virginia-highway-snow-crash?utm_source=chatgpt.com

God is going to plant people all over the earth in every occupation so that His splendor will be seen by all. Remember, it is your uniqueness that stands out, not your conformity to what the world thinks you should be like or look like. Like that machine operator, you were created to be someone's hero. God created you to be someone's answer, and your response will point them to Jesus.

CHAPTER THREE

THE SEASON OF PREPARATION

As we saw in the first chapter, God has a plan for each person that was designed before they were born. Their personalities and traits were all planned along the line of that destiny. And as I said earlier, no one knows their destiny when they are born. They discover it! **You Discover Your Destiny!**

Unique traits begin to appear even in babies. Their little personality and unique traits begin to show up, really, almost right away. Some babies are noisy, and some are calm. As they begin to age, we begin to see them drawn toward certain things that give us clues into their future. For instance, when our boys were very small, we decided that we did not want to introduce them to violent toys, like toy guns. But we were amazed as they would just pick up sticks and pretend they were swords. They were always in conquer mode, climbing and wrestling with each other.

But the girls wanted to cuddle baby dolls. No one told them to do that. That is what they wanted to do. They would also love to play house with their dolls and always wanted the boys to play house with them as the dad. But the boys usually did not want to do that. They were too busy building outdoors or fishing down at the pond. As they got older, more and more differences and interests started to emerge. These differences were all a clue to the destiny that God had planned for them.

Even though there are definite indicators of the direction a child might take, I believe the revelation of someone's destiny can only be gained by knowing the One who created them. Take driving a car, for example. The car is full of gas, the engine is running, and you are behind the wheel, but just not sure where to go and how to get there. Until you give the GPS the address, you are stuck. Even though all the elements required for the car to move forward are there, without the detailed instructions of where you are going, you are going nowhere, except possibly in circles.

I tell people that when you give your life to Jesus, God begins to unravel the mystery of you, to you!

I can see signs as I look back at my life. I see small indicators of what I liked and an interest in Bible stories inspired by my grandparents, who were Christians. However, most of what God had made me to be was buried under insecurity, fear, and inferiority. I was extremely shy growing up. I was born with the cartilage in my ears not formed correctly. My ears did not lie back against my head; they stuck straight out. If you will take a moment and feel your ear, you will find that it bends and lies back against your head. Imagine that your ear had no bend in it and your ear stuck straight out. Well, that is how my ears were, sticking straight out. And let me tell you, kids notice things like that, and they can be cruel.

I was called "big ears" all through those elementary years, which caused me to withdraw emotionally. Besides that, I was also overweight and a little chubby. My feet also turned inward, and I had to wear corrective shoes for years. These shoes were not your everyday shoes, so everyone noticed. They were black and white, which I never liked, and seemed to point to my turned-in feet. Because of these things, I was very shy and didn't want to draw attention to myself. This is how I lived for years.

I can remember, in sixth grade, I was walking down the hallway talking to a friend, not knowing my sixth-grade teacher was behind me. As I stopped to go into my class, she said, "So you can talk!" Because of my ears and the teasing, I always sat in the back of the class and never raised my hand to answer questions. Kids will make fun of you for just about anything that is different about you: your clothes, your accent, the color of your hair, just about anything and everything. So, I withdrew, and I fell in love with being outdoors where there were no people. But here is a truth you might as well know: you cannot hide from God; He will always work to keep moving you towards what He created you to do.

YOU CANNOT HIDE FROM GOD, HE WILL ALWAYS WORK TO KEEP MOVING YOU TOWARDS WHAT HE CREATED YOU TO DO.

My parents built a pizza restaurant in our little town, and I started working there when I was fifteen. I was the one who made the dough and worked in the back room putting together the pizzas before they went into the ovens. I was fine with that, but eventually, my parents needed some help waiting on customers, and I began to ring out the customers. Surprisingly, I found that I really liked working with the customers who came in. We lived in a very small town, and I eventually got to know most of the people who came in.

One day, a man came in who said he was an evangelist and was holding a revival down the street at a small Methodist church. Nothing unusual about that, but he said something that caught my attention. He said, "And Jesus is still doing everything He was doing while He was here on the earth." I grew up in a denominational church and found it to be somewhat boring, although I had prayed to Jesus when I was in fifth grade at their VBS. But I cannot say I saw a miracle there or God doing things. I had never heard someone say that Jesus is still healing or still doing miracles today. So when this guy stopped by the pizza shop, I was intrigued. He invited me down to the church, and out of curiosity, I said I would come.

I knew a couple of the kids who went to that church since they worked for me at the pizza shop. So, I went, and surprisingly, I found the service to be uplifting, and his message was very compelling. I could not explain it, but the presence of God was there, and that night is when my life changed. Even though I had prayed to Jesus as a fifth grader at the VBS, this was different. Everything in me wanted to follow Jesus after that night. I fell in love with reading the Bible and going to church. In fact, I made that little Methodist church my church and started going there any time the doors were open.

While there, I would hear some of the ladies talking about miracles and the power of the Holy Spirit. I could not help but overhear them talking about the power of God. I found out they held a ladies' Bible study at 10:00 a.m. on Thursday mornings, and although I was not a lady, I asked them if I could come. They gladly said I was welcome, even though I would be the only male there. So, on Thursdays, I went to the Bible study almost every week. They continually talked about something they called the Baptism of the Holy Spirit, but I had never really heard of this, so I was hungry to learn more.

Then, one week, they were all excited about a big meeting coming up in Columbus that was going to be about the Baptism of the Holy Spirit. This meeting was being held by a group called Women's Aglow, an inter-denominational organization that taught and encouraged people to receive the Baptism of the Holy Spirit. Again, although I was not a lady, I asked them if it was all right if I went. They said sure and were excited that I wanted to go. So, I went down to the meeting and found hundreds of women who were all so excited about the Holy Spirit.

After some brief singing, a woman got up and began to teach about the Baptism of the Holy Spirit. She taught how God has not changed, and that the power of the Holy Spirit was given to the church to do the works of God, just as Jesus had ministered. I was mesmerized by what she was saying, and all of it backed up by the Scriptures she was reading. As I sat there listening, I felt the presence of God like I did the first night I went to the Methodist church. As the woman who was teaching concluded her message, she then asked if anyone wanted to receive this Baptism. If so, they were invited to come up to the front and she would pray for them to receive it. Of course, I responded immediately.

As the lady laid her hands on me, I felt the presence of God so strongly. Then, words that I did not understand began to come into my mind and then out of my mouth. During the previous teaching segment in the service, the lady said that all of the nine gifts of the Holy Spirit had not passed away but were for the modern-day church. She made it clear that this Baptism of the Holy Spirit was different than salvation: where the Holy Spirit comes in you, and you become one with the Father. This was an anointing that comes upon the believer; an enduement of God's power to be a witness for the Kingdom of God.

> *But you will receive **power** when the Holy Spirit **comes on you;** and you will be my witnesses in Jerusalem, and in all Judea and Samaria, and to the ends of the earth.*
>
> —Acts 1:8 (NIV)

Boy, was I excited. At the time, I was helping lead a small group at the church for teens, which met together on Sunday nights. We would have a Bible study, then play some games, and just spend some time together. I could not wait to tell the kids what had just happened. I wasn't in charge of the group as I was only nineteen myself, but I helped organize and host it.

Well, that Sunday night, I told the kids to sit down in a semi-circle on the floor. The pastor was there and he sat next to me. I told the kids what had happened and how I had received the Baptism of the Holy Spirit and spoke in tongues when God's Spirit came on me. Of course, I knew very little about how to explain it, but I remembered a couple of the Scriptures that the lady had mentioned in her teaching. Of course, I just mentioned the one I remembered the most.

> *But you will receive **power** when the Holy Spirit **comes on you;** and you will be my witnesses in Jerusalem, and in all Judea and Samaria, and to the ends of the earth.*
>
> —Acts 1:8 (NIV)

After I offered a brief explanation, the best I could, I told them to bow their heads as we were going to pray to receive the Baptism of the Holy Spirit. I did not know what I was doing, but I was just trying to follow what the lady did and said when she prayed for me. The kids all bowed their heads, and I prayed. As I was praying, I began to hear laughing, crying, and languages I did not know. As I looked up, about nine to ten of the sixteen or eighteen kids who were there were speaking in tongues. Some were laughing, crying, and shaking under the power of the Holy Spirit. One thing I noticed right away was that the ones who had received the Holy Spirit had a glow on them. I was shocked, to tell you the truth. It was about then that the pastor, who was sitting beside me the whole time and hadn't said anything to me up until that point, tapped me on the shoulder and said, "I need to talk to you."

He motioned for me to follow him to a room not far away. When we got to the room, he told me that he was not going to have this in his church. He told me it was of the devil. I was a little confused by that statement. I had not told the kids what to do or say, and I knew it was the Holy Spirit on them, not the devil! That was a tough week. I was not one who wanted to do anything wrong, and I was confused as to what I had done wrong. The next weekend, I sat in the back of the church with all the youth. I usually sat up front, but I sat in the back that Sunday as I did not know how the pastor felt about me sitting up front with everything that had happened. But things were about to get crazier.

In our services, we always had a moment of silent prayer before we said the Lord's Prayer. That Sunday morning, as we were having our normal silent moment of prayer, suddenly, someone tapped me on the shoulder. I was sitting on the end of the pew, near the middle aisle, and someone was standing there tapping me on the shoulder. As I looked up, it was one of the youths who had been baptized in the Holy Spirit the previous weekend. I did not know why he would be standing during the quiet moment of meditation. But as I looked at him, I saw that he had that same glow on him as he did the previous Sunday night when he received the Baptism of the Holy Spirit. I then knew that something was going on. He said, "Let's go." I thought to myself, "Is he serious? Go where?" He realized I had no idea what was going on. So, he said that his mother, who was very sick and was facing a surgery to fuse five vertebrae in her back, was up front, and he wanted to go and pray for her.

He had just learned the previous week that the power of God was available to do miracles, and he wanted to bring that to his mother. He was an only child and his father usually wanted nothing to do with coming to church. So, I followed him to the front of the church where his mother was sitting in the second row. She was a very small, petite woman, and I thought that we could just walk up and pray over her for a minute. I thought the pastor would understand. But that was not what happened!

I was in shock as her son just picked her up and carried her to the front of the church and sat her down right in front of the pastor. Then he began to pray out loud in tongues for her. Of course, by this time, the quiet moment of meditation was certainly over. As I turned toward the congregation, all I could say was that speaking in tongues was in the Bible and that his mother was sick and he wanted to pray for her. Well, his mother was healed right there! What a day that was! Everyone was talking about her being healed in church, but there was quite a stir about him praying in tongues as well.

I am telling you this story to illustrate how, once I completely gave myself to Christ at the Methodist church, God began to show me the path toward my destiny. The power of the Holy Spirit changed everything. I found myself more excited about the Lord than ever. Although I did not see a different future or path for myself yet, I was excited. I was still working for my dad at the pizza shop, but things were about to change. I began to tell all the kids that I worked with about the Lord. I think before it was over, all of them came to know Jesus, and we had some pretty wild experiences there as the Holy

Spirit began working in all of us.

I remember one of the first kids there who wanted to know Jesus asked me to pray with him. He asked me how to be saved, and I told him that the second chapter of Acts says if anyone calls on the Lord, they shall be saved. I had never really led someone in prayer for salvation before, but the Bible was plain: whoever called on the Lord would be saved. So, I had Dave sit down in a folding chair in the back room where I made the dough. After I prayed for a bit, I told Dave to just call on Jesus. Nothing happened; Dave did not say a thing. I repeated my instruction, "Dave, just say the name of Jesus." Still nothing. I told him again to call on the name of Jesus. Again, nothing. I was confused why he was not following my instructions. But then I noticed that he was shaking all over. And then, as if he was trying to talk but something was holding his mouth shut, with some effort, he blurted out, "Jesus." At that, the peace of God came over his face, and he was free.

The next day, I saw Dave driving toward me. We were about to pass each other, but he slammed on his brakes and pulled over on the road. I knew he wanted to tell me something, so I pulled off the road. He ran over to my car and told me that after he left the pizza shop and was driving home, he noticed an oval-shaped cloud on the road ahead of him. There was no fog that night, but there was this oval-shaped cloud hovering over the road. At first, he was hesitant to drive into it. But as he was thinking it was just a strange bit of fog, he drove in. He said as he drove into the cloud, it was like he had gone to a different country. The trees were huge with silver leaves, and there was beautiful singing in the cloud. But the biggest thing he noticed was a tangible peace like he had never felt before. Then, in just a moment, he drove out of the cloud.

All the kids started asking about God and how to be saved. It was awesome. I did not know it then, but my heart to share Jesus with people started showing up. In fact, I started a Bible study at 1:00 a.m. at the pizza shop for all the kids in town who had nothing to do. Again, no one asked me to do this, it came naturally to me.

A few weeks after I was baptized in the Holy Spirit, it was my birthday, and I had planned to have a birthday lunch with some friends. At the dinner, the host asked me to pray over the meal they had prepared. As I bowed my head to pray, I felt the Holy Spirit come on me just as it had when I was at the Women's Aglow meeting. It got so strong that I asked to be excused. I did not know what to do. Behind me was the screen door to the backyard, and I told them I would be right back.

WHEN GOD CALLS US, HE THEN HAS TO EQUIP US AND MENTOR US TO HAVE THE ABILITY TO ACCOMPLISH WHAT HE HAS FOR US.

As I went out the door, the power of God got even stronger. Suddenly, I saw a picture of a room. The room was full of people sitting in folding chairs. The windows were dark, meaning it was dark outside. I saw myself holding a Bible, standing in front of the people. Then I heard in my spirit these words, "I am calling you to preach my Word!" I heard these words three times, then the anointing lifted. I kind of staggered back into the house and told them what had happened. I said, "I think I have just been called to preach!" At that moment, I really did not know what that meant. I was not told that I was going to pastor a church or preach as an evangelist, or what I was to do. But I knew the direction God had for me: I was to preach!

There comes a moment when you know the direction you are to go. It may not be a ministry position. It could be to launch out and start a company or go to college to learn a specific trade. I call this moment a glimpse, just a glimpse. God does not show you the entire picture yet, He shows you just enough to prompt you to take the next step in that direction. He never gives us the whole picture. You can call it a calling, a strong passion toward a direction, or simply, you just know the direction to go. But it is important you know the difference between being called and being sent. When God calls us, He then has to equip us and mentor us to have the ability to accomplish what He has for us. The process of preparation is a tedious one for sure, but the key is not to move ahead of God in this season. You will know when it is time to step out.

I believe that every Christian has a God-ordained direction. To achieve and reach that destiny, there is a process of cleansing and training that you will go through before God can show you the entire picture.

> *In a large house there are articles not only of **gold and silver,** but also of wood and clay; some are for **special purposes** and some for **common use**. Those who cleanse themselves from the latter (sin) will be instruments for special purposes, made holy, useful to the Master and prepared to do any good work.*
>
> —2 Timothy 2:20–21

Notice, both the common and the specially-purposed vessels are in the same house. They are both Christians, but not everyone will pay the price to be used for God's

THERE IS ALWAYS TIME BETWEEN THE CALL AND STEPPING INTO DESTINY.

special purposes.

There are articles of gold and silver in God's house, made for special purposes, made holy and useful to the Master, and prepared to do any good work. Before you can be considered for any good work, you must be prepared. Like gold, you must be purified, made holy and qualified before the Lord to receive that special purpose God has for you. I am not talking about salvation here; everyone who calls on the name of the Lord will be saved. But not everyone will pay the price of obedience to qualify for handling God's big assignments. On top of that, God has to posture you into a position to receive that assignment. Obviously, this is a process that takes time.

For me, the time it took between God calling me to preach until I actually stepped into my destiny that He showed me that day, was twenty-one years.

No, you did not read that incorrectly. It was twenty-one years! As great as Joseph was, it was thirteen years from the time he had the dreams of his future at home with his brothers until he was in Egypt, second to Pharaoh. It was forty years from the time that Moses ran from Egypt until God met him at the burning bush with his instruction to go before Pharaoh and demand the release of the Hebrew slaves. What about

Jesus? He was thirty when He began His ministry. There is always time between the call and stepping into destiny. This gap of time is where I want to focus our attention because this is where most people quit. Even Jesus had to submit to instruction and patiently wait until He was ready to step out.

Every year Jesus' parents went to Jerusalem for the Festival of the Passover. When he was twelve years old, they went up to the festival, according to the custom. After the festival was over, while his parents were returning home, the boy Jesus stayed behind in Jerusalem, but they were unaware of it. Thinking he was in their company, they traveled on for a day. Then they began looking for him among their relatives and friends.

When they did not find him, they went back to Jerusalem to look for him. After three days they found him in the temple courts, sitting among the teachers, listening to them and asking them questions. Everyone who heard him was amazed at his understanding and his answers. When his parents saw him, they were astonished. His mother said to him, "Son, why have you treated us like this? Your father and I have been anxiously searching for you."

"Why were you searching for me?" he asked. "Didn't you know I had to be in my Father's house?" But they did not understand what he was saying to them.

Then he went down to Nazareth with them and was obedient to them. But his mother treasured all these things in her heart. **And Jesus grew in wisdom and stature, and in favor with God and man.**

—Luke 2:41–52 (NIV)

Jesus had to submit to His parents, and by doing so, the Bible says He grew in wisdom and stature and in favor with God and man. If Jesus had to submit to the training and preparation process, you can be sure we all do.

For the Israelites, it was the wilderness that God used to teach and train them. Looking at them as an example, we can see a very common method that God uses to bring forth the gold in our lives. He moves us away from familiar influences where all we have is Him to depend on. There was no food or water in the desert, and Israel had to depend on God each day for the manna.

He humbled you, causing you to hunger and then feeding you with manna, which neither you nor your ancestors had known, to teach you that man does not live on bread alone but on every word that comes from the mouth of the Lord.

—Deuteronomy 8:3 (NIV)

He gave you manna to eat in the wilderness, something your ancestors had never known, to humble and test you so that in the end it might go well with you.

—Deuteronomy 8:16 (NIV)

God had to train them to rely on Him. Their future would require them to fully trust what He said. Which, of course, they failed to do and thus never entered into that promise. We can read these stories looking back on the nation of Israel and judge their unbelief, but so many people do the same thing. They refuse to allow God to lead them into the unknown.

How many times does God want to give us the great future that He has for us, but we fail to receive that direction because we quit the training process?

Let's review the Scripture I mentioned in 2 Timothy again; such a great truth.

> *In a large house there are articles not only of gold and silver, but also of wood and clay; some are for special purposes and some for common use. Those who cleanse themselves from the latter will be instruments for special purposes, made holy, useful to the Master and prepared to do any good work.*
> —2 Timothy 2:20–21 (NIV)

Two things stand out: God wants to make us into gold and silver, and that happens when we are cleansed from the impurities of sin and unbelief and learn to stay steadfast. Then we can qualify for God's special plans for our lives. So how does that happen? HEAT! The impurities must come to the top to be skimmed off. We must be stripped clean of all of our trust in ourselves and learn to trust and follow God.

CHAPTER FOUR

THE PREPARATION STAGE IS HARD; DON'T QUIT!

God will move you toward your destiny, but there is a price of obedience and perseverance needed to get there.

Yes, it was exciting to know that God had a plan for me. I was to preach His Word. But there was much to do before that could happen. God told me He wanted me to go to college! That's right. I couldn't believe it. Instead of sending me out to preach, God said, "Go to college." Why? Well, let's be honest, I basically flunked out of high school. They did let me graduate, but just barely. I didn't like school. Instead of being diligent with my classwork, I spent many days fishing instead of going to class. When I was in class, I did not learn much. Not because my teachers did not try to teach me, they did. Let me give you an example of how rotten my attitude was toward school. When the teacher would hand me a test, I would simply just hand it back and say that I did not want to take it. He or she, in frustration, would put a big "0" on it, but I did not care. I did not like school, and I did not like being there.

Yes, I had an attitude problem in high school, I will admit to that. And because of my attitude and lack of discipline, I graduated with a 1.3 average. And this is the guy that God was calling to preach His Word? No, this would never work. God is smarter than that. God had a lot to work into me and a lot to work out of me before that would ever happen. But just after high school and after being baptized in the Holy Spirit, I felt led to go to a one-year local Bible school. But unlike my days in high school, I was excited to go because I was going to learn about the Bible, which I admit, I did not know much about.

I enjoyed that year going to school and still working at the pizza shop. I got straight A's, which was something I had never done before, and it was awesome. Nothing really changed after I finished that year in school. I did not really have any direction as to what I was to do next. But a couple of months later, that changed.

I felt an urgency to spend some time in prayer one Sunday night, and as I did so, the Lord spoke to me and said I was to go to Oral Roberts University. What? Go to college? But wait, I heard that ORU had a very high scholastic requirement to get in, and I knew that my 1.3 average would not qualify. I hesitated to move on this, but God's leading to go just got stronger. So, finally, after arguing with God about it for a while, I filled out the application and sent it in with my transcript. I also wrote a letter telling them that I was not really plugged in during my high school years, but I had given my life to Jesus after leaving high school. I also sent them the transcript from the Bible school that I went to with straight A's, hopefully indicating the change I had after being born again.

A month went by, and a lady called and asked me some questions about my story. After about thirty minutes of explaining how I was changed and that God was calling me into the ministry, she said, "Well, you are right. You do not qualify to come here, but I am willing to give you a try." Later, I found out that ORU turned away 2,000 students that year in the freshman class, and I knew that it was God's favor on my life that moved the school to make that decision. It is interesting that God led me to take that one year of Bible school. I believe those straight A's spoke with evidence of the change in my life to the ORU administrator.

A week later, I received the acceptance letter, and as I read it, I almost panicked! Oral Roberts was very strong on the whole spirit, soul, and body concept. He believed that our bodies are the temple of the Holy Spirit, and we should do our best to honor God by keeping them in shape and healthy. The letter said that when I got on campus, the first thing I needed to do before registering for classes was to go to the gym and be weighed. I needed to weigh 209 pounds or less to be allowed to register for classes. At the time, I weighed 235 pounds. Well, what did they expect? I ran a pizza shop for the last few years.

Wow, that was tough. Now what? How was I going to lose that much weight? I then realized that the administrator who had called me was smart. She said I did not qualify to come, so she wanted me to prove that I would do what it took to get there. As you can probably already guess, I was not the disciplined type. Our pizza shop stayed open until 1:00 in the morning. Then, after closing, a lot of us would drive into Columbus and go to White Castle. They made these little cheeseburgers that I just loved. Well, I would usually order eight of them! Then I would go home and be in bed by about 3:00 a.m. It was no wonder I was out of shape and fat. But my life was about to change. Not only would I have to become disciplined with my studies at college, but I would also have to become physically disciplined as well.

The lady said nothing on the phone about my weight when she talked to me concerning my acceptance into the college, and I was concerned that I would be unable to accomplish such a huge goal in time. I really did not know where to start. About this time, running started to get popular, so I thought I would try that. But within a week, I had shin splints so bad I had to quit. So, I basically just stopped eating. I changed what I was eating, stopped going to White Castle, stopped eating our pizza, stopped eating dessert, and slowly, but surely, the weight began to fall off.

Leaving for Tulsa was tough. I had never really gone many places before this trip. I think I had only driven two or three times out of state. I was driving a 1969 Fiat 850 coupe at the time. The best example that you could compare it to would be just a bit bigger than a Smart car. Essentially, it was a motorcycle engine put in a car. I can't say that I was totally confident that it was up for the long trip, but it was all I had.

I had never left home before and was a little apprehensive about venturing out that far from home on my own. I can remember the feeling I had pulling out the morning I left. I looked back at my home in the rear-view mirror with a tear in my eye. I had no cell phone in those days, so I was on my own for sure. But after driving 16 hours, I made it to campus! The week before I was to leave for Tulsa, I weighed 212 pounds. The day I left, I weighed really close to 209 pounds. When I got there, I hit the 209-pound mark exactly!

My first year of college was extremely difficult as I was missing much of what I should have brought with me from high school. In my freshman English class, we had to write a paper. I thought I did pretty well with it. But when I got it back, the teacher had put a really big "F" on the front page and a statement that said, "Is it possible that you even went to high school?" That is how bad it was. I had to have a tutor help with my English that year. That is just an example of my struggle to finish this assignment that God had given me. Let's face it, God is not stupid; He needs His preachers to at least be able to write. There were so many times that I thought this was really just too hard. The pressure was there all the time. An interesting side note was that after I wrote my first book, the professor emailed me and said, "Is it possible that this is the same Gary Keesee that I had in class?" Yes, it is. And to date, I have written over twenty books. God is good!

I worked three part-time jobs to have money for gas, insurance, my car payment, and other expenses. One of my part-time jobs was going in to work at midnight, helping to prepare newspapers for delivery. I worked at the school café and some other interesting places. On top of that, ORU required you to exercise every week! In fact, you had to keep track of the exercise you did and how long you did it. If you failed to do this, you could not graduate. But that was not bad for me. In fact, it changed my life! Really!

When I arrived at ORU, I could barely run a mile, but as I continued to work at it, I got up to three miles. As my weight continued to decline to 180 pounds, I was able to run ten miles. During my years at ORU and even past ORU, I would always run three to five miles, four days a week, and I found out that being in shape was awesome!!!! It was like being born again. I loved to exercise. I also took up bike riding, which I still do three or four days a week now, and I am 70 years old. In fact, I have never stopped exercising since I left ORU. I have to admit that learning to love exercise and being near or at my proper weight was the greatest thing that ORU gave me besides my wonderful wife, whom I met there the year I graduated. ORU was a great experience, tough but great. I graduated with a bachelor's degree in Old Testament and a Business minor.

As I approached graduation, I began to pray about what I was to do next. Strangely, I did not hear God say anything. So, I thought that I should at least get a job with a church. After all, I was called into ministry. I applied to several churches, and they all turned me down. Still nothing from God. By then, I was in my own apartment with a couple of other guys, living off campus, and I had managed to find a job installing draperies and mini-blinds. I really had no direction and was wondering if I should head back to Ohio or stay in Tulsa. That is when I met Drenda! Wow, she was smart and beautiful. I began to think that maybe I needed to stay in Tulsa! We worked together at the Floors and Windows store, and sometimes she would go with me on an installation. I need to give you some background on what happened next, as I was about to face one of the hardest decisions of my life.

As you know, I was running one of my dad's pizza shops for a number of years when God called me to go to ORU. I hired and trained the manager who would take over my job when I left. Now, unexpectedly, my dad

I WAS CONVINCED THAT GOD HAD THE NEXT STEP FOR ME, I JUST DID NOT KNOW WHAT IT WAS.

called and told me that the manager was resigning and asked if I wanted to come home and take over the pizza shops. That was a hard call, because everything in me wanted to say, "Yes, I would love to come home and do that." I told my dad that I would call him the next day and let him know.

At the time, I had nothing going on. God had not spoken to me about direction, and I was lonely living with two other guys. But at the same time, I left that job in the pizza shop to follow God's call on my life. I knew I could not go back.

Although God had not spoken to me, I just knew I could not go back to the same thing I was doing before. I was convinced that God had the next step for me. I just did not know what it was.

Drenda and I had a time of prayer that night, and we both felt that I was not to go back to Ohio. The next day, I called my dad and told him of my decision to stay in Tulsa. He asked me what I was going to do, but I had no answer. "I do not know, Dad, but I do know that God brought me here, and He has something for me to do." My dad, who was not a believer, really did not understand. He meant well, I knew that. But I also knew I could not go home. Could I explain it? No, not really. I just knew that I could not go home.

I am not sure how many days it was after that phone call that Drenda stopped by. She had rarely stopped by my apartment since we worked together and saw each other every day, and we were not what you would call "boyfriend and girlfriend." But one evening, she stopped by to drop something off. Just then, I heard God say, "She is your wife!" I was sure I heard God right. It was so loud in my spirit that it was as if someone was saying it loudly in my ear. I did not say anything to her about what I had heard. But it would not leave me.

Over the next few days, I was sure that she was my wife. We had not dated. We only worked together, and she was my friend, but I was sure I had heard correctly. So, on March 10, at 1:31 p.m., I asked her to marry me. Amazingly, she said,

"Yes." We had never dated. We were just friends, and we are still friends, and I found out we make a great team. She is by far the best thing that has ever happened to me. God is faithful. Now I had my partner in life, and we were excited to see what God wanted us to do.

CHAPTER FIVE

IT GETS HOT IN THE FIRE!

Let's look at our Scripture again:

> *In a large house there are articles not only of **gold and silver,** but also of wood and clay; some are for special purposes and some for common use. Those who cleanse themselves from the latter will be instruments for special purposes, made holy, **useful to the Master and prepared to do any good work.***
>
> —2 Timothy 2:20–21 (NIV)

Paul is saying that if a person cleanses himself from sin and is tested in the fire of obedience, then they would be as gold, pure gold with the dross skimmed off. They can be trusted in special assignments because they will be steadfast, not trusting in themselves but trusting in God. They will not quit when the heat is turned up. I wish there were an easier way, but the dross does not rise to the top of the gold and silver unless it goes through the fire.

THERE IS NO SHORTCUT TO YOUR DESTINY! BEING FAITHFUL IS THE "SHORT" CUT.

We have been talking about the process of cleansing that God uses to bring to our attention the things that we need to abandon and cleanse from our lives. Most of this happens in the preparation phase when no one knows our name; thank God for that.

I had to choose to be obedient when God called me to ORU and lose twenty-six pounds to qualify for acceptance. Not only did I have to go to ORU when God called me, but I also had to finish my degree before I could move on. Sure, I did not like studying, but that is what God said to do. He opened the door to accomplish that and provided the finances so I would not have to carry school debt after finishing. So many people try to go around the hard things, always trying to find a shortcut. But in God's Kingdom, there is no shortcut.

There is no shortcut to your destiny! Being faithful is the "short" cut.

There is no use in asking God for a different plan. Once He has spoken to you, there is no use in asking for a way out of the pressure. There is no option two or option three available. And if you quit, He will bring you back right around to a similar assignment until you finish and pass the test.

Once I passed the test of going to college and finished it, which was the hardest thing I had ever done in my life up until that time, God gave me my wife. And although obeying and going to college was hard, things were about to go to a whole other level of hard. Now there was two of us, and I would need Drenda to pass the next test.

While I was living with the two guys in the apartment in Tulsa, my roommate received a book in the mail that his brother thought was interesting. It was titled, *Life Insurance: The Great National Consumer Fraud*, by Venita Van Caspel. I was puzzled why his brother would send him a book like this, as he was a Hebrew major and really had no interest in life insurance. He just set it aside and said I could look at it if I wanted to. Well, one day I saw it sitting in the apartment, and I picked it up, curious as to what could be wrong with life insurance. I owned a life insurance policy, which I bought when a schoolmate came by one day and sold me a $25,000 whole life policy, selling it as an investment for my future. So, I was curious as to why the author said life insurance was a fraud.

I know it sounds boring, but when I picked up the book just to casually take a look at it, I couldn't put it down. She was right, based on her data, whole life insurance is a fraud. She explained how cash value life insurance was usually sold as a savings plan, as well as providing a death benefit at death. But there was a problem with trying to combine both benefits in one policy. If you just need death protection, then the simplest and cheapest way to buy it is to buy what is called term insurance. There is no cash value built up, it just pays the face amount of the policy to the beneficiary upon death. Let me give you a simple illustration of what I am talking about.

Let's assume you are a 35-year-old, non-smoking male in good health. For $500,000 of death benefit with a ten-year level premium policy (it does not expire in ten years, the price just goes up), you would pay $245 annually. If you bought a policy that built up cash in the policy for a $500,000 face amount, you would be paying $2,480 a year. Both of these quotes come from the same company, by the way. Take a good look at these numbers; both of these quotes pay out $500,000 on death. Why would you want to pay $2,480 when you could have the same death benefit for $245? Secondly, if you bought term, you could invest the difference in the price in your IRA account and get a tax break. This is a very simple comparison, but I think it points out the problem.

Another issue is if you want to take some of your money out of your cash value policy, you have to borrow it and pay interest on your own money. Yes, I know there are all sorts of life insurance policies out there, and some are extremely complicated, but what I have just shown you bears out that term insurance is always the cheapest way to buy death protection. So, reading her book, I was shocked to find these things out. About two weeks later, as I was thinking about what I had just read, I received a call. The guy on the phone was calling to invite me to a meeting about a new company focused on selling only term insurance. I asked him how he knew of me and how he got my number. He said that he got the number from a company I had applied to, but did not get the job. I guess he knew someone who worked there and asked if he could call those whom they had turned down. I thought it was more than interesting that I had just read that book. I decided I would go since I was curious to find out what this company was all about.

When I went to the meeting, amazingly, the company was exposing all of the things I had just read about cash value life insurance. They were on a crusade to tell people to buy term and invest the difference. They even mentioned the book that my roommate had let me read. I was very excited about what the company was doing and gave serious thought to joining it. The downside was that it was a sales position that paid 100% commissions, and I had never been interested in selling anything in the past. But I just could not get this company out of my mind. As I contemplated going to work for the company, I did not look at it as sales, I looked at it as a crusade to expose the insurance company's fraudulent strategies. But I had just graduated from ORU, and I could not forget the call of God on my life. On the surface, this opportunity, although intriguing, did not really seem to be in line with that assignment. But I felt such a pull toward being involved with the company that I began to pray and ask God if, in fact, I was to go in that direction.

I had just asked Drenda to marry me and was going to visit her family in Georgia the following weekend. It was great to meet her parents and brothers, and she wanted to take me to her church that weekend, which I was looking forward to. When the weekend came, I found the church to be exciting, and I enjoyed meeting her pastor and her friends there. But after the service, a lady walked up to me and said that she had a word from the Lord for me. I really did not have a lot of experience with the gifts of the Spirit personally, but I asked her to tell me what the Lord wanted her to tell me. She said, "You are looking at a job in the financial field, and the Lord said it will involve these ten points." She then listed the ten points, which matched exactly what I was looking at. She said, "The Lord says to take the position. He is in it." Well, I knew that word had to be from God. It was so exact, and I had not told anyone that I was looking at that position. She matched every aspect of the position I was looking at in Tulsa in detail. So, when I got back to Tulsa, still a little surprised and maybe a little confused as to why I was not going into the ministry yet, I signed up for the position.

Now, here is something that I want to make sure you remember: although I went to college and finished it, I was still scared to speak with people, let alone sell anything. But there was something inside of me that was pulling me toward that position that I just could not deny. And now that Drenda's friend confirmed that direction, I was ready to go. The first step was to take and pass a state life insurance licensing exam, which I did. Next, I went out with my manager on a few cases where I got to watch the entire client process, which I found to be fascinating. After my manager signed off on my initial training, it was then up to me to begin setting up my own appointments.

I can remember my first night trying to set up an appointment. Since I had been a student in Tulsa, I really did not know many people outside of the school, so I asked my boss at the Floor and Windows store if I could call back some of the clients that I had installed for him. He said I could, which I thought was amazing in itself. I went down to the Floors and Windows store, walked into the office, and began to pull the files that I had installed. Now was the moment of truth. I had to talk to a client on my own. I was so nervous! I had to get up enough courage to actually make the call, and I will have to admit it was a very intimidating task for me to do.

I sat there at the phone, wrestling with myself for over three hours. I finally did make some calls and actually had two people agree to meet me. Believe it or not, one of them actually bought a policy from me! Wow! Although it was hard, I knew that the Lord had directed me in this direction. Again, I really had no answer as to why God had directed me in this direction when I was called into ministry. Later, it became very clear why He did, which I will share with you later in this book.

When Drenda and I got married, we decided that I would stay with the company, living on commissions. Our bills were not very high, and we thought we could do all right staying there. Besides, it offered some great income if you went into management and built a team. Living on commissions is a very loose explanation of how we lived, because you had to sell something to have a commission to live on. I dreaded making those phone calls. I knew that I had to have the following week set up with evening appointments by Saturday, or I would not make much, if any, money at all. So, every

Saturday, I would go to the office to make phone calls to the referrals I had obtained that week. Almost all of my appointments were in the evenings since that was when everyone was home, and my goal was to have between eight and ten appointments a week. It would take me several hours to get those appointments set, and sometimes most of the day. I dreaded Saturdays for that very reason.

As we started out as newlyweds, we had to have a good car, a home, furniture, and everything you need to set up a home. Unfortunately, we used debt to do almost all of that. Our mindset was that it was only one more sale. Well, the one more sale did not always come in, so we would use credit cards to make up the difference. Before long, we began to fall behind on our bills, and life became very stressful. You know, it is a very strange mindset in sales. I found myself thinking that the next week will be a great week, and I can catch up on these bills and pay these credit cards off. But then it wouldn't be a great week, and we would borrow more money.

I dreaded making phone calls so much that one day I told Drenda I just did not like doing it and wanted to do something else. Of course, since we ran our own schedule with the financial company, I did not need to actually quit, I decided to work at the financial business part-time and find a full-time job that would offer more security. My days were basically free, so I signed up with a landscape company to work during the day. The temperature in Tulsa was averaging 100 degrees, and yes, I could then add something else to the "I hate to do" list. I hated digging ditches more than phone calls! I told Drenda that I had to make the financial business work; I could not dig ditches in this heat. I knew, besides working hard, I had to get into the management side of the business. That was where the bigger money was.

Drenda jumped in and helped me make a few calls, and she talked to a guy who wanted to join my team. He was my first hire. I asked Drenda if she wanted to continue to make more calls for me but she said, "NO", in a very clear, decisive voice. She said she wanted me to learn to make those calls if this business was, in fact, going to pay the bills. I had to learn to make the calls myself, especially if I was going to train new sales reps to do it. Of course, she was right, but you can't fault me for trying!

I am telling you, I died a million deaths making those calls and living on commissions. But slowly they got a little easier, and I started hiring and training reps. Drenda and I felt that with hard work, we could achieve the top sales contract in the company: Regional Vice President. That position offered the highest sales contract, and the company would allow you to open your own office. This position was the goal of everyone who came into the company. This is where a person could really start making good money.

Well, in our second year, we made it! The company had a big meeting, recognized me, and I was promoted. I should have been excited, but I was so depressed from the stress that, again, I did not want to work for the company anymore.

I hated the stress of being in debt and living on commissions. Although I totally believed in what I was doing, I was tired of fighting the insecurity of 100% commissions. The fact of the matter was that if I did not make my phone calls, I was basically unemployed every week.

The stress of making that happen was really starting to affect me. It just was not working. I had to find something else to do, something with some security. The next morning, after the big promotion event, a friend who was one of my roommates when I was in college just stopped by unannounced. I had not heard from him for a couple of years. I do not know to this day how he found where I lived, but I was glad to see him. He asked me how I was doing, and seeing the promotion plaque sitting on the coffee table, he asked about it. So, I told him about my promotion and then said, "But I have decided to leave the company." He acted shocked and began to tell me that I could not do that after finally reaching the RVP position. He went on and on about not quitting. Then he got up and left, and I have not heard or seen him since that day.

It was so strange that he would just show up and talk to me for about an hour about why I would be crazy to quit the business. After I thought about what he said and the fact that I had not heard God tell me to quit, I stayed with it. Things did not get much better after I became an RVP. I was doing better, but still in debt and living month to month. Looking back, I know it was God that he stopped by. Just like I know it is God that you picked this book up.

You are destined for greatness if you will just persevere in the fire, and trust me, I know what it is like to persevere in the fire! But I also know how great it is when you have paid the price, and you win. And let me say this: winning is so much better than you have ever thought. It is worth any fire you may go through. Just remember, quitting what God told you to do, is not an option. He has great plans for you!

One day, I was out jogging, and the Lord spoke to me. God did speak to me about small things from time to time, but never about direction, ever since He led me into the financial field. There were so many days that I prayed that I could do something else, but He would never give me the green light to do it. As I was jogging one day, He said, "I am calling you now to Ohio, where you will do your end-time work." He said nothing of leaving the financial business and nothing really specific about ministry, just that in Ohio, Drenda and I would be doing our end-time work. I did not know what that end-time work was. I always had the memory of the vision I had when He called me to preach, and I was wondering if I would find that fulfilled in Ohio. I was not sure, but God usually just gave me the next step, not the entire picture.

QUITTING WHAT GOD TOLD YOU TO DO IS NOT AN OPTION. HE HAS GREAT PLANS FOR YOU!

We were so excited to move back to Ohio, where I had family. I continued with the financial company when I moved, but by that time, financially, we were not doing well at all. To make the move, we had to sell our house, and the problem was that Tulsa was in a major recession. Foreclosures were happening all over the place. We were falling behind on our mortgage payment at the time, so we went into the bank to find out what our options were since we were moving.

When we sat down with the manager of the bank and told her our situation, the first thing she said, while pointing to a large stack of papers, was, "These are all foreclosures. We do not want any more. So, we will let you sell your house for whatever it appraises for, and we will write off the difference. I will give you six months to sell it, or we will foreclose. Secondly, during this six-month period of time, I will allow you to pay one-half of your normal mortgage payment. But if the house does not sell, the other half of these payments will be added back onto the loan balance." Lastly, she told us that this payment arrangement would not show up on our credit report. Wow, we were so thrilled for a way out and to move to Ohio.

We signed up with a real estate company, and they did not show it once during the first five months. We began to get a little nervous about finding a buyer. We were convinced the real estate company did not work at selling our property, so we decided that we would sell our house ourselves. I called the real estate company, canceled our contract with them, and told them we are going to try to sell the house ourselves. Drenda made up one ad for the Tulsa paper and advertised an open house. A lady came that day who bought the house, with cash! Well, that was amazing!

I thought when we got to Ohio, things would be better. In many ways, they were, but financially, they weren't. Things got worse. You may say, "Gary, why are you telling me all this?" Because I want you to see how God works, how He leads us into and through tough things, so we will learn how to trust Him. You see, when God led Israel through the wilderness, He knew what was ahead. There were walled cities, giants, and armies that would stand against them when they crossed over the River Jordan. But until they could trust Him with the small things like finding water when it looked like there was no water, trusting God for food when all they saw was sand, trusting God's leadership team, and submitting to Moses without grumbling, God knew they would not trust Him when the enemy was standing face-to-face against them.

Everyone will go through similar training. As I mentioned, Moses had his 40 years in the wilderness before God spoke to him about his destiny. Joseph went through betrayal in his family, false accusations from Potiphar's wife, and years in prison for something he did not do. But in every case, as we look back at where these people ended up, it was all necessary to prepare them for their ultimate destiny. Looking back is always 20/20. It made sense that God led me to go to college before I went into the ministry. I was so deficient in so many things that would be essential to my success. Being so shy around people, it made sense that God would thrust me into sales, where I was forced to talk to people every day, just to pay the bills. God knew where I was heading. I, of course, didn't. And that is where we need to trust Him.

ONLY GOD KNOWS THE TEST THAT WE ALL MUST PASS BEFORE WE CAN BE TRUSTED WITH THE TRUE PRESSURE FROM THE ENEMY IN A LIFE-AND-DEATH CONTEST.

The title of this book infers that there are three battles that you must win to step into your destiny: the private battle, the public battle, and the battle to occupy. But before we engage in these battles, we must be in the season of preparation, where we learn discipline, obedience, and submission. Each of these is essential and will be tested to a higher degree in the actual personal battles we must win when no one knows our name. In a way, much of what we learn in our time of preparation is part of the personal battle we must win as well, but it is tested at a much more intense level. Only God knows the test that we all must pass before we can be trusted with the true pressure from the enemy in a life-and-death contest. But there is grace for the test. Although I had made progress, I did not yet sense a call to preach, so I knew there was more that I had to learn. God was not finished preparing me for my destiny. There was more fire, there was more dross that had to come out before God could trust me to do what He asked of me. I thought school and starting my own financial business were hard, but I was yet to face much harder things.

People ask me, "Why can't God just tell me about my destiny?" Because you would probably blab it, and then Satan would pick up on it and bring pressure against it when your character is not mature enough to stand.

Remember the story of Zechariah, John the Baptist's father? He was a priest and one day while ministering in the temple, an angel appeared before him and told him that he and Elizabeth were going to have a baby. He also told them that they were to call him John. Zechariah did not believe the angel, so the angel closed his mouth, and he was unable to talk until after the baby had been born. Why? He would have messed up the entire plan of God if he were able to talk. That is why God will not tell you all the details until you are mature enough to handle those details with faith. He shines just enough light on your path, showing you the next step, which is all you need. Just keep moving forward one step at a time. Let me give you an example of this.

> *We do, however, speak a message of wisdom among the mature, but not the wisdom of this age or of the rulers of this age, who are coming to nothing. No, we declare God's wisdom, a mystery that has been hidden and that God destined for our glory before time began. **None of the rulers of this age understood it, for if they had, they would not have crucified the Lord of glory.***
>
> —1 Corinthians 2:6–8 (NIV)

Let me paraphrase what Paul is saying here: if Satan had

known the plan of God, he would not have crucified Jesus. He would have changed tactics. This is true for us as well, as I have been saying. If you do not know your destiny and future, guess what? Satan doesn't either. But he is always trying to discern what that path might be, so he can come against it. Let me say it a different way. Why was Jesus born in a manger like some pauper? Exactly. God was not going to tip Satan off. Satan does not know everything, and he is not everywhere. When Herod heard of the birth of Jesus, he wanted to kill the child, but he could not find him. So, he just killed all the males under the age of two to be sure he got Him. But he was too late because Joseph and Mary had already left for Egypt with the boy. Satan can only react to what he sees. He has no revelation. He is in complete darkness. We, however, are children of the light, and God leads us away from Satan's plans. The Lord's Prayer teaches us that we can trust God to lead us around Satan's roadblocks.

This, then, is how you should pray:

"Our Father in heaven, hallowed be your name, your kingdom come, your will be done, on earth as it is in heaven. Give us today our daily bread. And forgive us our debts, as we also have forgiven our debtors. ***And lead us not into temptation, but deliver us from the evil one."***

—Mathew 6:9–13 (NIV)

If we stay in tune with God, He promises to lead us around Satan's plans to hinder our destiny and purpose.

But we must be wise to the tactics of the enemy. He will always try to intercept God's plan for us. He will play on our weaknesses, insecurities, and fears to tempt us. God knows that we need to face those fears and weaknesses **BEFORE** we step into the fight with Goliath or face the giants and walled cities of the promised land.

I remember visiting one of my friends who had a job at an aircraft manufacturing plant. He was allowed to show me what he did there. His job was to shine a special light on aircraft parts to verify that there were no cracks or weaknesses in the metal. That was his entire job, all day long. The special light would reveal the hairline cracks that we could not see with our eyes. Of course, we all would want those cracks spotted before those parts were used in an airplane, and then have that part fail in flight. It is better to search for these weaknesses before the actual flight. So it is with us. God wants to expose our weaknesses before we get to our destiny.

GOD KNOWS THAT WE NEED TO FACE THOSE FEARS AND WEAKNESSES BEFORE WE STEP INTO THE FIGHT WITH GOLIATH.

Let's say that, as a man, you have trouble with pornography. Do you think God could trust you in a big assignment? Satan knows your weaknesses. He has been watching you for a long time. He knows how to set you up. If you are going to be the gold that God can trust, you must be immune to temptation. Now, of course, I think every man notices a pretty woman; that is nature. I am talking about being tempted by a pretty woman toward a lustful encounter. If God put you in a high-level role, Satan, knowing your weakness, will try to set you up with an encounter to tempt you to sin. And once you give in to it, you come under his jurisdiction, where he can steal, kill, and destroy. Now, if you do find yourself missing the mark, you need to learn to repent and repent quickly and shut the door. There is no condemnation in Christ, but there is wisdom. Stay away from temptation. Let me help you understand this topic of temptation.

I have never drunk alcohol. I am not tempted at all to be around it. It means nothing to me. There is no temptation or desire toward it. Everything stays silent in my head when I see it. There is no voice speaking to me about it. I can walk down the alcohol aisle in the grocery store, and there is complete peace. But that is not the case when I walk down the bakery aisle. I can be easily tempted by it. Listen carefully to this verse.

> *No temptation has overtaken you except what is common to mankind. And God is faithful; he will not let you be **tempted** beyond what you can bear. But when you are **tempted,** he will also provide a way out so that you can endure it.*
>
> —1 Corinthians 10:13 (NIV)

God is not going to put you someplace where you do not

have the grace and wisdom to withstand being tempted beyond your ability to withstand it. So, if you want a promotion, you will have to be trustworthy. This is huge! Usually, most of this type of training is done in the private battle or the preparation phase of your training.

Like the aircraft parts that my friend inspects, God will need any cracks to be located and dealt with before He can move you on toward your destiny. When I buy gold coins, they always say 99.9% pure gold. All the dross has to be out of that gold before it is formed into the coin. We have to be able to be trusted by God with uncompromised allegiance, complete trustworthiness, and always available for the Master's use. How you handle the smallest assignment will reveal your heart toward the Lord.

> **Flee** *the evil desires of youth and pursue righteousness, faith, love and peace, along with those who call on the Lord out of a pure heart.*
> —2 Timothy 2:22 (NIV)

> *Those who want to get rich fall into temptation and a trap and into many foolish and harmful desires that plunge people into ruin and destruction. For the love of money is a root of all kinds of evil. Some people, eager for money, have wandered from the faith and pierced themselves with many griefs. But you, man of God,* **flee** *from all this, and pursue righteousness, godliness, faith, love, endurance and gentleness.*
> —1 Timothy 6:9–11 (NIV)

What is Paul's advice to Timothy? FLEE!

Are you tempted or do you flee? That is the question, and that is what must be the case when you are on a top mission for God. Either you are not tempted, or you flee.

A TEST OF LOYALTY AND SUBMISSION IS ALWAYS VITAL BEFORE PLACING A PERSON IN A POSITION.

These are the kinds of tests that you must grow through and pass.

Let's say that your weakness is chocolate bars. Would God send you on a mission into the Hershey's factory? Probably not. God knows our hearts, and we all must guard our thoughts, what we look at, and meditate on.

Paul told Pastor Timothy to test people before they were placed into leadership. This was not a test of their ability; no, it was a test of their loyalty and obedience.

> *They must first be **tested**, and then if there is nothing against them, let them serve as deacons.*

> —1 Timothy 3:10 (NIV)

A test of loyalty and submission is always vital before placing a person in a position. If someone is found not to pass the test, that does not mean they are finished forever. No, it just means they are still in training and not quite ready for the assignment. Yet so many leaders promote only on skill and talent and have reaped the chaos and confusion that can bring. The Holy Spirit will train you. After all, He is more invested in you occupying your destiny than you are. Do not let the Lord's discipline be something that you despise. God loves you enough to correct you. Welcome it and heed it, for your future depends on it.

CHAPTER SIX

THE PRIVATE BATTLE

When we think about David, we automatically think of Goliath. But to understand that event with Goliath and David, we need to look deeper than just the day that the two of them met. Taking some time to examine what took place before that event took place gives us huge clues as to how God works with us in our training toward destiny. So, let's take a look at David's history and see if we can find some keys.

When David was talking to King Saul about Goliath and offering to go up against him, we need to know, first of all, that this was not his first time facing danger and not his first time seeing deliverance. Victories won in the public arena are rarely, if ever, the first battle someone has. Just as a wide receiver might catch the winning pass, we all know that behind that catch, there were a lot of catches that took place in private, many of them dropped. God trains the same way. The private battle is usually within ourselves or a battle that does not involve a lot of publicity, where our weaknesses are exposed and dealt with before we actually go to game day. David had the same kind of training, and so will you.

> *David said to Saul, "Let no one lose heart on account of this Philistine; your servant will go and fight him." Saul replied, "You are not able to go out against this Philistine and fight him; you are only a young man, and he has been a warrior from his youth." But David said to Saul, "Your servant has been keeping his father's sheep. When a lion or a bear came and carried off a sheep from the flock, I went after it, struck it and rescued the sheep from its mouth. When it turned on me, I seized it by its hair, struck it and killed it. Your servant has killed both the lion and the bear; this uncircumcised Philistine will be like one of them, because he has defied the armies of the living God. The Lord who rescued me from the paw of the lion and the paw of the bear will rescue me from the hand of this Philistine."*
>
> —1 Samuel 17:32–37 (NIV)

David was confident because his faith in God had been tested, as well as his courage to face tough challenges. This was not his first life-threatening fight. Let's face it, grabbing a bear or lion by its hair is not something I would want to do. Although he slew both the lion and the bear, the greatest victory we see is that he was so committed to the trust given to him that he risked his life to honor it. This is the story that stands out. David was persuaded that God was with him, and he was confident not only in his ability but in the God he served.

Unless you are responsible with the small task, you will not be promoted to a bigger task. You may say, "Well, no one knows, I can cut corners, and it is not a big deal," but God is watching. He is the one who promotes. I mean, is a sheep more important than David's own life? No, of course not. But when you care about the small assignments with the same integrity and effort that you would with the big assignments, that is when you can be trusted. The bear and the lion were David's personal battles. No one was there but him. He could have easily made excuses for the loss of one sheep.

UNLESS YOU ARE RESPONSIBLE WITH THE SMALL TASK, YOU WILL NOT BE PROMOTED TO A BIGGER TASK.

But David also knew that the battle you fear to face today will be back tomorrow. He knew that the bear and the lion, if allowed to steal an animal, would not stop coming back unless it was killed. His faithfulness with the sheep and his trust in God qualified him to represent God against Goliath. God knew what He wanted to do there, but He had to have a man who would believe Him and give Him jurisdiction to accomplish it.

If you were God, would you want King Saul, who was quaking in fear at the sight of Goliath, leading your people? Or would you want David, who was saying, "Let me at him!" and has proven that he can handle it? I think it is obvious. So many people talk a good game, but you need to be the David, the one who steps out in faith and goes for it. Do not be afraid to engage in the private battle, whether it is a bad habit, some hidden sin, or just living an apathetic life. God's grace is only engaged when you step into it. If you study the battle between David and Goliath, you will see

SO MANY PEOPLE TALK A GOOD GAME, BUT YOU NEED TO BE THE DAVID, THE ONE WHO STEPS OUT IN FAITH AND GOES FOR IT.

that David ran toward Goliath. This threw Goliath off, as David came at him with no weapons. Remember, Goliath thought David was coming at him with a stick, but did not see the sling. This supernatural battle plan took Goliath out. God has your battle plan as well. Learn to hear His voice in the private battles so God can use you in the public battles.

> *I assure you that there were many widows in Israel in Elijah's time, when the sky was shut for three and a half years and there was a severe famine throughout the land. Yet Elijah was not sent to any of them, but to a widow in Zarephath in the region of Sidon.*
>
> —Luke 4:25–26 (NIV)

Underline the word "sent" in the above Scripture because I want to come back to it in a minute. The complete story that Jesus was referring to is written in 1 Kings 17.

Some time later the brook dried up because there had been no rain in the land. Then the word of the Lord came to him: "Go at once to Zarephath in the region of Sidon and stay there. I have directed a widow there to supply you with food." So he went to Zarephath. When he came to the town gate, a widow was there gathering sticks. He called to her and asked, "Would you bring me a little water in a jar so I may have a drink?" As she was going to get it, he called, "And bring me, please, a piece of bread."

"As surely as the Lord your God lives," she replied, "I don't have any bread—only a handful of flour in a jar and a little olive oil in a jug. I am gathering a few sticks to take home and make a meal for myself and my son, that we may eat it—and die."

Elijah said to her, "Don't be afraid. Go home and do as you have said. But first make a small loaf of bread for me from what you have and bring it to me, and then make something for yourself and your son. For this is what the Lord, the God of Israel, says: 'The jar of flour will not be used up and the jug of oil will not run dry until the day the Lord sends rain on the land.'"

She went away and did as Elijah had told her. So there was food every day for Elijah and for the woman and her family. For the jar of flour was not used up and the jug of oil did not run dry, in keeping with the word of the Lord spoken by Elijah.

—1 Kings 17:7–16 (NIV)

When first reading this story, it may seem harsh that the prophet would take the widow's last meal. But doing so saved her life!

Read verse 13 again:

> *Elijah said to her, "**Don't be afraid**. Go home and do as you have said. **But first make a small loaf of bread for me** from what you have and bring it to me, and then make something for yourself and your son."*
> —1 Kings 17:13 (NIV)

When he asked her to make him a loaf of bread before she did the same for herself, the flour came under God's jurisdiction when she obeyed. That gave God the legal spiritual jurisdiction to multiply the remaining flour.

> *So there was food every day for Elijah and for the woman and her family.*
> —1 Kings 17:15b (NIV)

Food for God's mission and food for the family; this is how it works today as well. But the real point of bringing up this story is the word "sent." **Elijah was sent to this woman**. To paraphrase Jesus, were there no other widows in Israel who needed help? This woman was not even in the nation of Israel. God qualifies people. He is looking for a person who will believe Him and do what He says. You must qualify to get the big assignments that God needs done on the earth.

Regarding what God said about David:

> *After removing Saul, he made David their king. God testified concerning him: 'I have found David son of Jesse, a man after my own heart;* **he will do everything I want him to do.'**
>
> —Acts 13:22 (NIV)

Was David destined to become the king of Israel? Yes, but only if he paid the price of obedience. David had to pay the price of winning the personal battle before he could be trusted in the public battle. No one thought much of him. His own father did not call him to the house when the prophet went to his father and told him to have all the boys come in, as one of them would be king. No, a shepherd was not a high calling of grandeur. But David was faithful when no one knew his name. Without proper understanding of how God works, many quit when they face the hardships of obedience when dealing with personal battles or learning to stay in faith while in the preparation stage.

Let me show you something very interesting. If you remember, Jesse, David's father, sent David down to the front line with some provisions for a few of his sons who were in Saul's army, which was lined up against the Philistines. This was where David heard Goliath ranting and raving against Israel. David heard some of the guys talking about the reward that King Saul would give to the man who took Goliath out, and he was intrigued. So, he continued to ask other men if that was correct.

Eliab, his older brother, heard David fraternizing with the men and lost his temper: "What are you doing here! Why aren't you minding your own business, tending that scrawny flock of sheep? I know what you're up to. You've come down here to see the sights, hoping for a ringside seat at a bloody battle!"

—1 Samuel 17:28 (MSG)

Eliab was the one that Elijah thought could be king when he first went to Jesse's home, but it is obvious now why he was not chosen. He belittled David for taking care of the family's sheep. Owning sheep was a sign of wealth for a family, providing wool for clothing and food to eat. The fact that Eliab called his family's sheep a scrawny flock revealed his lack of concern for his family and his lack of appreciation for David's care for them. God knew that if Eliab were made king, he would have the same lack of concern for God's sheep, God's people. But how

GOD IS WATCHING THE ATTITUDE OF YOUR HEART AND YOUR OBEDIENCE TO HIM, EVEN IN THE SMALL THINGS.

could Eliab have known that God was going to judge him unfit to be king by how he judged the importance and concern for his family's sheep? Again, I will tell you that God is watching the attitude of your heart and your obedience to Him, even in the small things. Your obedience to the small assignments reveals who you are and how you will handle the bigger assignments.

What about Moses? As we have already discussed, Moses was raised in Egypt, around government and the best that Egypt had. Although Moses had the pedigree, he would only be valuable to God if he did what God told him to do. But Moses had to pass his own private battles, like all of us.

> *The Lord said, "I have indeed seen the misery of my people in Egypt. I have heard them crying out because of their slave drivers, and I am concerned about their suffering. So I have come down to rescue them from the hand of the Egyptians and to bring them up out of that land into a good and spacious land, a land flowing with milk and honey—the home of the Canaanites, Hittites, Amorites, Perizzites, Hivites and Jebusites. And now the cry of the Israelites has reached me, and I have seen the way the Egyptians are oppressing them. So now, go. I am sending you to Pharaoh to bring my people the Israelites out of Egypt."*
>
> ***But Moses said to God, "Who am I that I should go to Pharaoh and bring the Israelites out of Egypt?"***
>
> ***And God said, "I will be with you***. *And this will be the sign to you that it is I who have sent you: When you have brought the people out of Egypt, you will worship God on this mountain."*
>
> —Exodus 3:7–12 (NIV)

Wow, this was a big test for Moses. He had been away from

Egypt for forty years at that point, and he knew enough to know that facing Pharaoh and demanding the slaves be set free was not child's play. He also knew how important the Hebrew slaves were to the nation of Egypt and that Pharaoh was probably not just going to let them go. He also knew his life was in danger by just going before Pharaoh since he had run away as a criminal in the past. He was gone for forty years after killing an Egyptian. God's demand is clear concerning what He wanted him to do. Yet Moses hesitates and says, "Who am I to go before Pharaoh?"

ALL THINGS ARE POSSIBLE FOR THOSE WHO BELIEVE!

That is a good question for any of us, and our answer has a lot to do with where we end up. If God is leading us to do something and we say right back to Him, "Who am I to do such a thing?" we're saying, "I can't do that!" Stop before you begin with all the excuses. Let's remember what God said. All things are possible for those who believe!!!

For those who believe! When did God say He would be with Moses? Not when he was just thinking about the idea. No, when he was actively carrying out the assignment that God gave him. You can look all you want before you ask for proof that God will show up, but you will see nothing except His Word. It is when you engage by faith in what God has told you to do that His grace and provision show up. So many times, God has led us to do big things when we did not have the money in the bank to do it. But it was after we said yes and actually set ourselves to accomplish it that the money showed up.

In Moses's story, he was still not sure about all of this, and turned his attention away from Pharaoh for a moment to give another excuse to God. He wondered out loud to God if the Hebrews would believe that he had actually heard from God.

> *Moses answered, "What if they do not believe me or listen to me and say, 'The Lord did not appear to you'?" Then the Lord said to him, "What is that in your hand?" "A staff," he replied. The Lord said, "Throw it on the ground."*
>
> *Moses threw it on the ground and it became a snake, and he **ran from it**. Then the Lord said to him, **"Reach out your hand and take it by the tail."** So Moses reached out and took hold of the snake and it turned back into a staff in his hand. "This," said the Lord, "is so that they may believe that the Lord, the God of their fathers—the God of Abraham, the God of Isaac and the God of Jacob—has appeared to you."*
>
> *—Exodus 4:1–5 (NIV)*

Moses knew what kind of snake he was messing with, which is why he ran from it. Most people believe that the snake was a King Cobra. The King Cobra is one of the world's deadliest snakes because the amount of venom it releases when it bites is enough to kill an elephant or twenty men. But God was telling Moses to pick it up by the tail! I have read numerous articles about picking up snakes, and the most common advice is to never pick one up by the tail, especially a poisonous one. It can curl up and bite you on the arm or hand or bite your leg. Yet God was telling Moses to do that very thing.

Key: God knew if Moses could not pick up the snake by the tail, which was dangerous, then he would never be able to have the courage to face Pharaoh.

God was showing Moses something else, even more important than the snake. If Moses picked the snake up by the tail and believed God to do so, it would turn back into a staff. The staff represents authority. Moses had a choice to run in fear from the assignment that God was giving him. If he would step into the assignment and pick it up, God's authority would be with him, protect him, help him on the journey, and nothing could harm him, even Pharaoh.

YOU MUST WIN THE PRIVATE BATTLE BEFORE YOU CAN MOVE FORWARD AND FACE A BIGGER, MORE INTIMIDATING ENEMY.

You will have to make the same decision. You must win the private battle before you can move forward and face a bigger, more intimidating enemy. Moses had to face his fear of the snake and instead put his trust in what God was telling him. Your destiny will require the same thing! It's the personal battle. The personal battle goes past the preparation phases of our training and moves into the application, training us to use our faith and apply what God is teaching us. In Moses's case, God had to reinforce the training, so he began with the snake: fear or authority?

> *As Pharaoh approached, the Israelites looked up, and there were the Egyptians, marching after them. They were terrified and cried out to the Lord. They said to Moses, "Was it because there were no graves in Egypt that you brought us to the desert to die? What have you done to us by bringing us out of Egypt? Didn't we say to you in Egypt, 'Leave us alone; let us serve the Egyptians'? It would have been better for us to serve the Egyptians than to die in the desert!"*

> *Moses answered the people, "Do not be afraid. Stand firm and you will see the deliverance the Lord will bring you today. The Egyptians you see today you will never see again. The Lord will fight for you; you need only to be still."*

> *Then the Lord said to Moses, **"Why are you crying out to me?** Tell the Israelites to move on. **Raise your staff** and stretch out your hand over the sea to divide the water so that the Israelites can go through the sea on dry ground. I will harden the hearts of the*

> *Egyptians so that they will go in after them. And I will gain glory through Pharaoh and all his army, through his chariots and his horsemen. The Egyptians will know that I am the Lord when I gain glory through Pharaoh, his chariots and his horsemen."*
>
> —Exodus 14:10–18 (NIV)

To set the stage, Moses has just led Israel out of Egypt and led them toward the Red Sea as God directed. When they came to the Red Sea, they were hemmed in on both sides by mountains and now by the Red Sea in front of them. To make matters horribly worse, Pharaoh had changed his mind about letting them go and was now coming after them. He found them trapped between the mountains and the sea. The people, of course, were panicking. It would have been a frightful thing to be trapped against the sea and find Pharaoh's army about to overtake you. But Moses freezes, and God has to rebuke him in verse fifteen because it seems Moses does not know what to do.

> *"Why are you crying out to me? Tell the Israelites to move on. **Raise your staff** and stretch out your hand over the sea to divide the water so that the Israelites can go through the sea on dry ground.*
>
> —Exodus 14:15–16 (NIV)

My paraphrase: "Moses, you have my authority. Do something about this situation!" It is the same lesson: fear or God's authority? Pick up the staff. Again, Moses had a choice to take his eyes off the problem and look to God or panic with two million people screaming in terror all around him.

Moses had to learn this lesson, and so do you! There are bigger giants and problems ahead. You must learn to use your authority in the private battle so you can exercise God's authority in the public battle.

CHAPTER SEVEN

THE PRIVATE BATTLE–PART TWO

As I have been saying, winning the private battle is required before God will move you on to the public battle. Let me lay out what I mean. Your private battle is just that; it is private. It is not usually public knowledge, but it is dealing with things that you must win against: a familiar sin, a bad habit, wrong mindsets, character flaws, and more. These are the things that the enemy would love to exploit and hold you back with.

> *Therefore, since we are surrounded by such a great cloud of witnesses, let us throw off everything that hinders and the sin that so easily entangles. And let us run with perseverance the race marked out for us, fixing our eyes on Jesus, the pioneer and perfecter of faith. For the joy set before him he endured the cross, scorning its shame, and sat down at the right hand of the throne of God.*
>
> —Hebrews 12:1–2 (NIV)

This is what God wants to see: throwing off those things that hinder and the sin that entangles you before He promotes you to a place of influence, which destiny always has attached to it. The Holy Spirit will deal with you and help you overcome these areas in your life that you need deliverance from. Drenda and I sure needed that! During my preparation season, the Lord led me to college because I played my way through high school. He led me into sales because I was so afraid to talk to people. Although there was much pressure and turmoil, I stayed with the financial business. I told you how God led us to move to Ohio to accomplish our end-time work. And again, I can say, I was not sure what that meant exactly. When God called me to preach His Word, He did not tell me how or where I would be doing that.

Ohio turned out to be tough. We brought all the debt we had with us from Tulsa. It was a mess. The stress was beyond measure for me. I had no idea how to escape the trap that I had put around me. Within a very short time after getting to Ohio, we had ten maxed-out credit cards, three finance company loans, IRS liens, two car loans, and we owed everyone money. We owed our parents, the dentist, the dry cleaners, friends, just about everyone. The stress was horrible, and it had a huge effect on my marriage, my family, and my health. We were attending a good church, but I did not know how to deal with all this from a spiritual standpoint. I could see answers in the Bible, but did not know how to bring them from the pages of the Bible and into our lives.

One day, I woke up and something was terribly wrong. It

seemed like my whole body was numb. My face and neck were numb. My arms and legs were numb. I could hardly stand or talk. I went to the hospital. They could find nothing wrong with me and said it was a panic attack. I had never even heard of a panic attack before that. Fear overtook my life. I began to notice that the panic attacks were more numerous when I ate sugar or had caffeine, so I began to watch what I ate, which did help some. But I was constantly having these panic attacks. I could not sleep and was tormented by horrible thoughts that I did not want to think, but I could not stop my mind from thinking them.

I was already a Christian, and I knew that this was not from God, but I could not break it. At that time in my Christian walk, I had never really had to wrestle with demons, although I had seen one once when I was praying for an unbeliever at my dad's pizza shop. But as far as dealing with demons, I really had no experience. I knew something was not right, and the doctors said there was nothing wrong with me, but I knew there was. I began to wonder if what I was going through was caused by a demon. A few weeks later, I found the answer to that question.

I had gone to church on a Wednesday night. Everything felt fine until I walked into the church. As praise and worship started, I felt that horrible feeling of fear and a panic attack. I did not know what to do, but I was desperate. So, I just walked up to the front where the pastor was as the security team tried to figure out who I was. One of the pastors on staff knew me and told the senior pastor that I was okay but that I had been going through some physical problems. The senior pastor walked toward me and said, "Well, the problem is that you have a spirit of infirmity tormenting you." He then rebuked the spirit in a loud voice, and I remember falling backwards. I lay there for a moment. Then, when I went to get up, I realized that I felt fine, completely normal for the first time in weeks.

We went to Pizza Hut after the meeting, and there was a strange song playing on the jukebox, which was irritating to me. Then suddenly, I felt that horrible fear come over me again. But this time, I knew that it was a spirit that was tormenting me. The following Wednesday, I spent extra time in prayer at home. During prayer, that fear left me again, and I was free, at least for a couple of hours. Then it came back. I was excited when I realized that this spirit responded to spiritual authority. So, I would rebuke it, and from time to time it would leave, but it always came back.

One morning, going into my office, the fear was unusually strong. I was so tired of this battle and was a little frustrated. But that morning, the Lord spoke to me and said, "You need to rebuke that thing and tell it to go. And when you do, pay no attention to your emotions, but just begin to thank me that it is gone." So, I went into the restroom where my secretary could not hear me, and I said, "Satan, I bind you, and I command this spirit of fear to leave, in the name of Jesus." Nothing changed, but I remembered what the Lord had said: to thank Him and to pay no attention to my emotions. I still felt sick when I walked back into my office. But I just kept thanking God that it had left. After about ten or fifteen minutes, the anointing of God came on me, I saw this black wispy cloud go up through the ceiling, and I was free!

Although the torment from the spirit of fear was gone, I was still having trouble with my reaction to sugar. Drenda and I heard about a conference that was being held at Oral Roberts University, and we thought we would go. One of the speakers was Benny Hinn, who would be conducting a healing night during the conference, and we thought we would believe God for complete healing in my body. To make a long story short, we went to the meeting, and Benny did pray for me with a powerful anointing! After he prayed for me, I could not get up off the floor. I remember a couple of guys came and lifted me up onto a chair. It was a while before I could get up. The anointing was so strong. But I was confused when I left the meeting because I still felt sick. I thought, *My goodness, the anointing was so strong, I should have been healed!* (This shows you just how immature I really was at the time, and I had a lot to learn about faith and how the Kingdom operates). When I woke up in the morning, just before I was fully awake, I had a dream. Well, really, it was just a Scripture that came up out of my spirit.

> *Therefore, I tell you, whatever you ask for in prayer,*
> *believe that you have received it, and it will be yours.*
> —Mark 11:24 (NIV)

At the time, I could not remember where this Scripture was, as I was still just waking up. So, I told Drenda about the

Scripture that God was telling me, and she said that it was Mark 11:24. As I was thinking on this Scripture, I finally saw what God was trying to tell me. Wait a minute, I do not have to have the proof that I am healed by waiting for the symptoms to disappear. If God says I am healed, then I am healed. I told Drenda what the Lord was showing me, and said, "We need to get some root beer!"

IF GOD SAYS I AM HEALED, THEN I AM HEALED.

There is a famous root beer stand in Tulsa that we went to when we were students, called Weber's Root Beer on Peoria Avenue. I said again, "Let's go get some root beer." Drenda knew, and I knew that in the past, if I had eaten something really sweet, my body would react with shakiness and sometimes numbness, and I would feel sick. When we got to the restaurant, I told them to give me one of those really big, iced mugs. Before I took the first sip, Drenda said, "I believe you are healed!" I said, "I am healed." When I drank that root beer, it was so good that I asked for a second mug. I drank both of them and had no problem, and have not had a problem since. I was healed!

God had to train me how to deal with that demon, and He continued training me how to use my faith and how His Kingdom works. I had to learn these things before He put me in a position of spiritual authority. There were things I would still need to learn to believe for, like the millions of dollars that God would require me to believe Him for that I knew nothing about at the time. But God knew.

These personal battles were intense, but they had to take place. I had to win them. But the biggest personal battle that I had to face was the one of my personal finances and debt!

All through the battle with my health and the spirit of fear, our finances were just horrible. Many times during this season, I just found it hard to focus and work. The phone calls from creditors kept coming, but there was no money to pay them. It got so bad that our refrigerator was empty, and the commission pipeline was almost empty. On one particular day, I was just so discouraged. I had exhausted everything I knew to do, including pawning my guns to raise some money. I was done. There was nothing I could do. I went upstairs to the little bedroom in the old farmhouse we were renting and lay across the bed, crying out to God for help. I was shocked that I heard Him answer me, not audibly, but it almost sounded that way. He first reminded me of a Scripture in Philippians.

> *And my God will meet all your needs according to the riches of his glory in Christ Jesus.*
> —Philippians 4:19 (NIV)

I told Him that I knew that Scripture, but it was not happening in my life. He quickly answered that it was because I had never learned how His Kingdom operated and that I was doing everything the way the world does things and not asking Him what to do. Yes, it was a rebuke, but it was an answer.

But I did not really know what He meant by "Kingdom."

I went and told Drenda what He had said, and we prayed together that God would teach us how His Kingdom operated. We did not have to wait long before He started teaching us.

That morning, the day that I had gone up into our bedroom crying out to God, an attorney, one of many who consistently called us trying to collect an outstanding debt. He called and threatened me with a lawsuit if I did not pay the $1,600 I owed them within three days. We had a real problem on our hands, and we did not know how to get the money that the attorney said we had three days to get. Neither did we know how to handle the lawsuit that was now going to be filed against us if we did not come up with the money in three days. "Lord, how do I get out of this one? The Kingdom?" Let me tell you what happened. Remember how the attorney said I had three days to get the money to him? I had none! That despair was what caused me to go to my bedroom and cry out to the Lord. I was in trouble!

The next day, I was headed to meet a client in the evening about his life insurance. By the way, in those days, I always parked my vehicle around the corner from my client's house, never in front of the house. The minivan that I was driving had a slight problem. When it started, it filled the driveway or street with white smoke, and I don't mean a little either. I just always felt it would not help business if I parked in my client's driveway and, upon leaving, filled the driveway with smoke. I assumed my credibility in the area of finances might be slightly affected since I was asking them to invest hundreds of thousands of dollars with me. This night was no different.

As I made my way from my client's home that night, I was horrified to see that the man was actually following me down the street to my van. He meant nothing by it, we were just talking. But I was a little concerned that he would hang around while I started the van. We continued talking as I got into my van. With the window down, I continued to talk, hoping that he would say good night and I could then act like I was doing something for a minute as he walked away, but he didn't. Finally, he did say good night, but he simply backed away from the van and stood there. I knew I was had.

I started the van, hoping maybe this one time it would not erupt in white smoke, but that was a wish that was not to be. Instantly, the air was filled with smoke that burned your eyes. The man motioned to me in a hurried way to turn off the van. He walked back over to the window and asked if I could put up the hood. He then went on to explain to me that he worked part-time as an auto mechanic, and he wanted to check something out. After a minute, he came back and said, "Just as I suspected, you have a busted head gasket. Drive the van home, and get it fixed immediately." I thanked him as I drove away, but his diagnosis meant nothing to me. I had no money to fix the van.

My office was only about six miles from my client's home,

and as I headed back toward my office, that familiar blanket of depression came over me. But as I was driving, I remembered what the Lord had said to me, and I began to talk to Him about my van. "Lord", I said, "I do not have any money to fix this van. I still owe money on it as well, and I cannot sell it broken. I just do not know what to do. Maybe it would be better if the van just burned up. That way, the insurance company would pay it off and I would be rid of it."

About three miles from my office, I noticed a bubble on the hood that I had not noticed before. As I watched, the bubble got bigger and bigger until, as I pulled into my office's parking lot, the bubble burst into a ball of flame. I was in shock. The entire front of the van was now engulfed in flames that rose six feet off the hood. I quickly ran into the office building and called the fire department. The next day, the van was totaled by the insurance company. They gave me a check which paid it off with enough left over to overnight a check to the attorney who had called me three days earlier.

Drenda and I were amazed. We did not know what to think. We knew that God was working for us and that something was changing. But our commitment to the Kingdom was about to be tested in a new way that would set our path for years to come.

After the van burned up, we were, of course excited, but we suddenly realized that we were without a vehicle. Although the van was now paid off and the credit card debt was paid, we had no money to purchase a new van. Upon hearing of the loss of our van, my dad called and told us that he wanted to help us get a new van. We were excited as we heard the news. So, my dad and I went to the local car dealership and found a van that Drenda and I liked. My dad said that he would give us $5,000 toward its purchase, which was about $17,000. That would leave us $12,000 to finance. I reluctantly filled out a credit application, and my dad co-signed for it. The dealership would let me know in the morning whether or not our application was accepted.

That night, we could not sleep. We knew that we could not take that loan. The Lord had just spoken to me about doing just such a thing. But with no vehicle, the pressure was there for me to bend and give in. After a horrible night of sleep, Drenda and I agreed that we just could not sign that loan paper. I called my dad and thanked him for his gracious offer, but we were going to decline. Next, I called the dealership and told them the same thing. They were also disappointed as the loan had been approved that morning, and the van was ready to pick up. Although we had no clue as to how God was going to help us with our van, we felt at peace about it.

During that time period, Drenda had been selling a few antiques she found at garage sales, etc. She had left a message for a man about buying several rooms of furniture that he had for sale a month before the van burned up, but had not been able to make contact with him. A couple of days after the van burned up, he called and agreed to sell three rooms stuffed full of furniture to Drenda for less than $1,500.

Drenda made an agreement with an auction company to sell the furniture for her and was able to negotiate her commission on the auction for a good used vehicle that the auction company owned, instead of cash. So now we had a good station wagon that was paid for, the credit card was paid off, and the van loan was paid off. Wow! So, this is how the Kingdom operates. At that point, we had proven to ourselves that God's system worked, and we committed ourselves to keep learning and using God's system of the Kingdom from that point forward. We then understood that God can meet needs without debt, and we were excited to continue learning and were believing God to pay all of our debt off, not just the van's debt. And of course, within a year, we had everything paid off.

As we began to study and pray about what the Lord told me, that I needed to learn how His Kingdom operated, I realized out that a kingdom is a form of government. It has a king whose leadership is enforced throughout the king's dominion through laws. This was probably the most powerful thing I had to learn: the Kingdom of God is a government. It has laws of operation that do not change. Like gravity, these laws work every time. If a person would foolishly say to you that they believe they could jump off the Empire State Building and just flap their arms and slowly fly to the ground, you would know that if they really did try that, the end result would not be good. Why do you know that? Because you understand the law of gravity, which does not change. If someone told you they could light a house, you would believe them because the laws of electricity have been discovered and explained in great detail. But when it comes to the Kingdom of God, people do not seem to know the laws of the Kingdom.

As Drenda and I began to study the Kingdom of God and started learning how the Kingdom operated, our lives changed drastically. There are so many stories that I could tell you, many of which are in my *Your Financial Revolution* series of books. But the van story was the first real evidence that we saw of the Kingdom.

AS DRENDA AND I BEGAN TO STUDY THE KINGDOM OF GOD AND STARTED LEARNING HOW THE KINGDOM OPERATED, OUR LIVES CHANGED DRASTICALLY.

When God told me the issue with my finances was my lack of understanding regarding the Kingdom of God, I was eager to find out what He meant. As I said, He showed me that His Kingdom is a government that operates by laws. But He also began to show us Scripture that verified that.

> *He will reign on David's throne and over his kingdom,* ***establishing and upholding it with justice and righteousness*** *from that time on and forever.*
> —Isaiah 9:7b (NIV)

Isaiah says that the Kingdom of God was established and is being upheld by justice, which means the administration of laws. Those laws enforce what the King declares over His Kingdom and its citizens, which is righteousness. Basically, what the King says is right. God taught me that if I learned those laws and mixed them with faith, they would work for me every time. In fact, the Bible confirms this in 1 John:

> *This is the confidence we have in approaching God: that if we ask anything according to his will, he hears us. And if we know that he hears us—whatever we ask—we know that we have what we asked of him.*
>
> —1 John 5:14–15 (NIV)

IF WE KNOW THE LAWS THAT GOD HAS PUT IN PLACE, WE CAN HAVE ABSOLUTE CONFIDENCE THAT WE WILL HAVE WHAT WE HAVE ASKED OF HIM IF WE ASK ACCORDING TO WHAT HE SAYS IS OURS.

When this Scripture mentions that God hears us, it is not talking about God audibly hearing us, although He does. It is speaking of God hearing the case, rendering justice based on His laws. So, if we know the laws that God has put in place, we can have absolute confidence that we will have what we have asked of Him if we ask according to what He says is ours.

Let me give you one more Scripture.

> *"Blessed are you who are poor, for yours is the kingdom of God."*
>
> —Luke 6:20b (NIV)

Again, the Kingdom infers government and laws. As citizens of the Kingdom of God, we have legal standing before God to enjoy every benefit the King has declared over His citizens.

> For no matter how many promises God has made, they are **"Yes"** in Christ. And so through him the **"Amen"** is spoken by us to the glory of God.
>
> —2 Corinthians 1:20 (NIV)

Drenda and I continued to study the Kingdom, and we saw so many things happen as we applied what we were learning.

One night, God gave me a dream that I had started a new company, one that was not completely unlike the one I was working with. But it was a company that would have the objective to share what we were learning about the Kingdom. As I began praying about that idea, I had a meeting with a client that God used to launch us in a completely new direction.

When I sat down with Dave and Sally, they seemed like your average, everyday family. They were in debt and trapped financially. They were just living paycheck to paycheck. When I began to talk about their debt, Sally was in tears. The stress was taking a toll on them. I told them my story and how God was showing me that there is a Kingdom way of living where the Holy Spirit will help us prosper, and we can stay out of debt. As I looked at their data, I knew that there was no sale there for me, but I took their data and told them I would look it over and see if there was anything I could do to help them.

As I was driving home from the appointment, I had an idea. I had a list of everything they spent their money on, so I planned on calling other vendors to see if I could find cheaper, less expensive options that could provide the same services they were using. This was before the Internet, by the way, and I had to do my searching by phone and the yellow pages. After a week of research, I found that if they changed some of the vendors they were using and switched to ones I had found, it would free up almost $600 a month. I then applied that freed-up cash flow to their debt structure, and I was in shock! My calculation showed they could be completely out of debt, including their home mortgage in less than seven years, without changing their income. I think it was around 6.2 years! I could not believe it. I ran the calculation over and over again and found the same answer.

So, I set another appointment with Dave and Sally and typed out a one-page report that showed this possibility. When I sat down with them and slowly went through the different ways they could save money and the impact that would have on their debt, they were in disbelief. They jumped up in tears and hugged me. They had hope. This was it!!!! This is what I wanted to do. I wanted to do for families what I had just done for Dave and Sally. So, I hired a computer programmer and designed a system that would input data and then spit out the completed financial results regarding freed-up money and the impact that freed up money would have on their debt. I called the company Faith-Full Family Finances. Implying that by faith, your finances will stay full. Years later, we changed the name to Forward Financial Group. We started that company, and it began to grow. Within a couple of years, we were completely out of debt. It has been over thirty years since we started that company, and it has grown over the years into a multimillion-dollar company.

The company became number one out of 5,000 offices in 1996 and 1997 with one of our insurance vendors. You would think that now that we were out of debt, we would take some time to relax and enjoy our success. But no, that was not God's plan. You see, being debt-free is not really a goal. Of course, it is in a way, but being debt-free in itself only removes a roadblock from your true goal, your destiny.

I can remember then, in the fall of 1995, hearing the Lord say to me, "Now, I want you to launch a church in your hometown of New Albany, Ohio, teaching my people what I have taught you." Another "I have no idea how to do that, Lord" conversation took place, but of course Drenda and I followed His directive. It had been twenty-one years since the Lord called me to preach. The local radio station offered us a room in their building to start our church, free of charge. The first meeting we had as a church was on a Wednesday night. As I stood before the people, which I think numbered about forty, I saw a familiar picture. I have seen this room before. It was the exact picture that the Lord gave me when He called me to preach twenty-one years earlier. The people sitting in folding chairs, the dark windows as it was night. The layout and furnishing of the room. I was in the right place!

I had been faithful in the private battle. I had been

WE HAD EVIDENCE THAT THE KINGDOM OF GOD IS REAL, AND IT WORKS!

faithful in the public battle, which was all the people I had testified to of our deliverance from debt, and many who were now following us in ministry. We had the fruit of God's Word, and it could be seen publicly. We had evidence that the Kingdom of God is real, and it works! I cannot even put into words how great it was to be out of debt. And then to see God's exact picture He gave me when He called me to preach come to pass, it was just amazing.

But there was still more to get done.

CHAPTER EIGHT

THE PUBLIC BATTLE

The easiest way to describe the public battle is to look at a couple of examples in the Bible. I have discussed in depth the private battle, but now the public battle comes before the third battle, the battle for occupation. It is important; essential!

Meanwhile, the Philistine, with his shield bearer in front of him, kept coming closer to David. He looked David over and saw that he was little more than a boy, glowing with health and handsome, and he despised him. He said to David, "Am I a dog, that you come at me with sticks?" And the Philistine cursed David by his gods. "Come here," he said, "and I'll give your flesh to the birds and the wild animals!"

David said to the Philistine, "You come against me with sword and spear and javelin, but I come against you in the name of the Lord Almighty, the God of the armies of Israel, whom you have defied. This day the

*Lord will deliver you into my hands, and I'll strike you down and cut off your head. This very day I will give the carcasses of the Philistine army to the birds and the wild animals, and the whole world will know that there is a God in Israel. **All those gathered here will know that it is not by sword or spear that the Lord saves; for the battle is the Lord's, and he will give all of you into our hands."***

As the Philistine moved closer to attack him, David ran quickly toward the battle line to meet him. Reaching into his bag and taking out a stone, he slung it and struck the Philistine on the forehead. The stone sank into his forehead, and he fell face down on the ground.

*So David triumphed over the Philistine with a sling and a stone; **without a sword** in his hand, he struck down the Philistine and killed him.*

David ran and stood over him. He took hold of the Philistine's sword and drew it from the sheath. After he killed him, he cut off his head with the sword.

*When the Philistines saw that their hero was dead, they turned and ran. **Then the men of Israel and Judah surged forward with a shout** and pursued the Philistines to the entrance of Gath and to the gates of Ekron. Their dead were strewn along the Shaaraim road to Gath and Ekron. When the Israelites re-*

turned from chasing the Philistines, they plundered their camp.

David took the Philistine's head and brought it to Jerusalem; he put the Philistine's weapons in his own tent.

As Saul watched David going out to meet the Philistine, he said to Abner, commander of the army, "Abner, whose son is that young man?" Abner replied, "As surely as you live, Your Majesty, I don't know." The king said, "Find out whose son this young man is."

—1 Samuel 17:41–56 (NIV)

At the time of this event, David had already been anointed by Samuel to be king over Israel. No one knew that, of course, except David's own family. To be king, David would need the people's hearts and allegiance.

WHEN PEOPLE SEE YOUR PUBLIC VICTORY, THEY WILL WANT TO KNOW WHO YOU ARE AS WELL.

This is the purpose of winning the public battle.

Whatever you build, whether a ministry or a business, it will take people. And not just people, but people who are loyal to you. You can't buy loyalty, although many try. You earn it.

No one knew who this kid was! Neither the king nor Abner had any idea, but they wanted to find out. When people see your public victory, they will want to know who you are as well. The anointing on your assignment will draw people to you. And that is what happened with David.

> *David left Gath and escaped to the cave of Adullam. When his brothers and his father's household heard about it, they went down to him there. All those who were in **distress or in debt or discontented gathered around him, and he became their commander**. About four hundred men were with him.*
>
> —1 Samuel 22:1–2 (NIV)

When his father and brothers heard where he was, they came. When four hundred were in distress, in debt and discontented, they came. Why? Because they saw their answer. They wanted to follow David. King Saul was shaking in fear. The nation was about to be taken over, but David believed God and saved the nation. But did they follow him into a fancy high-end hotel? No! They followed him into a cave! There was nothing in the cave except David. What I mean is, there was nothing in the cave that would draw people to the cave except one thing: David was there. David did not say, "I am passing around a legal pad for those who want me to be their life coach! Just sign up, my rates are very good." No! They followed David into a cave! The Bible says he became their leader. No, he did not solicit them to follow him. They just followed him. Listen, when people see the victory in your life, they will follow you too. Did it turn out well for those who followed David? I think so. They were called David's mighty men of valor!

When David was collecting the money to build the temple, he gave a large amount out of his own treasury. God had told David that he would not be the one who would build the temple. His son, Solomon, would be the one who would build it. But David had the responsibility to gather the money and materials to build it. David himself gave a great amount of wealth toward the project, but David's men also gave to the temple, as recorded in 1 Chronicles 29:7. This is what I want you to see:

> *Then the leaders of families, the officers of the tribes of Israel, the commanders of thousands and commanders of hundreds, and the officials in charge of the king's work gave willingly. They gave toward the work on the temple of God five thousand talents and ten thousand darics of gold, ten thousand talents of silver, eighteen thousand talents of bronze and a hundred thousand talents of iron. Anyone who had precious stones gave them to the treasury of the temple of the Lord in the custody of Jehiel the Gershonite. The people rejoiced at the willing response of their leaders, for they had given freely and wholeheartedly to the Lord. David the king also rejoiced greatly.*
>
> —1 Chronicles 29: 6–9 (NIV)

Let me go over what they gave one more time and put the value in today's dollars next to it:

190 tons of gold ($30 billion)
380 tons of silver ($516 million)
675 tons of bronze ($4 million)
4,000 tons of Iron ($1 million)

$30,521,000,000.00 total

Well, one thing is sure: they were not in debt any longer! They were nobodies when they went into the cave, but they became wealthy when they followed David. It does make a big difference who you are following.

Moses had to win the personal battle, but he also had to win the public battle. Those two million Hebrews needed to hear and see God's anointing on him. When they saw those plagues come on the Egyptians just as Moses said, they were ready to follow him anywhere. And when the Red Sea parted, and the Egyptian army was destroyed before their very eyes, no more talk was needed. They were all in. This gave great confidence to the people who were following Moses and Aaron.

Joseph had to win the personal battle, forgiving his family for selling him into slavery. And after he was betrayed and falsely accused by Potiphar's wife and spent all those years in prison, he could have become bitter, a complainer, and mad at God. But he was faithful through all of those years to honor God and do his best.

There is a pattern to how Joseph won the personal battle.

*The Lord was with Joseph so that he prospered, and he lived in the house of his Egyptian master. When his master saw that the Lord was with him and that the Lord gave him success in everything he did, **Joseph found favor in his eyes and became his attendant.** Potiphar put him in charge of his household, and he entrusted to his care everything he owned. From the time he put him in charge of his household and of all that he owned, the Lord blessed the household of the Egyptian because of Joseph. The blessing of the Lord was on everything Potiphar had, both in the house and in the field. So **Potiphar left everything he had in Joseph's care; with Joseph in charge, he did not concern himself with anything except the food he ate.***

—Genesis 39:2–6 (NIV)

He handled Potiphar's affairs as if they were his own, with excellence! Again, in prison, we find the same good report concerning Joseph.

*But while Joseph was there in the prison, the Lord was with him; he showed him kindness and granted him favor in the eyes of the prison warden. [22] So the warden put Joseph in charge of all those held in the prison, and **he was made responsible for all that was done there.** [23] The warden paid no attention to anything under Joseph's care, because the Lord was with Joseph and gave him success in whatever he did.*

—Genesis 39:20b–23 (NIV)

Again, Joseph handled prison affairs with integrity and excellence. When Pharaoh had a dream he could not interpret, he called on Joseph and said, "I have heard it said of you that when you hear a dream you can interpret it."

GOD KNOWS WHERE YOU ARE. TRUST HIM. Oh, that is how it works, friend. What do people say about you? Do not wallow in self-pity in the trying times of obedience. It is a setup that God will turn for your good. God knows where you are. Trust Him. Joseph had a good reputation with Potiphar, who did not really believe his wife. I believe he knew that the accusations were false. Joseph also had a good report around the palace since Pharaoh did not hesitate to bring him out of prison and eventually put him in charge of the whole country. If there had been a bad report concerning him, I do not believe that Pharaoh would have done that. He had such a good reputation in the prison, such that he actually took over running the prison.

I love it when Pharaoh said, "I have heard it said of you!" That is such a powerful statement. Joseph was winning the public battle even while he was in Potiphar's house and in prison. The reputation he earned while he was a nobody is what gave him good standing before Pharaoh.

Never underestimate the influence you have in any situation. It may look hopeless, but God is watching, and He is your promoter. If you are faithful and hold true in those dark times, God will honor you. You just need to pass the test. Let me show you a parable that Jesus told, which underscores what I'm saying:

> *Again, it will be like a man going on a journey, who called his servants and entrusted his wealth to them. To one he gave five bags of gold, to another two bags, and to another one bag, each according to his ability. Then he went on his journey. The man who had received five bags of gold went at once and put his money to work and gained five bags more. So also, the one with two bags of gold gained two more. But the man who had received one bag went off, dug a hole in the ground and hid his master's money.*

> *After a long time the master of those servants returned and settled accounts with them. The man who had received five bags of gold brought the other five. "Master," he said, "you entrusted me with five bags of gold. See, I have gained five more."*

> *His master replied, "Well done, good and faithful servant!* **You have been faithful with a few things; I will put you in charge of many things.** *Come and share your master's happiness!"*

> *The man with two bags of gold also came. "Master," he said, "you entrusted me with two bags of gold;*

see, I have gained two more."

His master replied, "Well done, good and faithful servant! **You have been faithful with a few things; I will put you in charge of many things.** *Come and share your master's happiness!"*

Then the man who had received one bag of gold came. "Master," he said, "I knew that you are a hard man, harvesting where you have not sown and gathering where you have not scattered seed. So I was afraid and went out and hid your gold in the ground. See, here is what belongs to you."

His master replied, "You wicked, lazy servant! So you knew that I harvest where I have not sown and gather where I have not scattered seed? Well then, you should have put my money on deposit with the bankers, so that when I returned I would have received it back with interest.

"'So take the bag of gold from him and give it to the one who has ten bags. For whoever has will be given more, and they will have an abundance. Whoever does not have, even what they have will be taken from them. And throw that worthless servant outside, into the darkness, where there will be weeping and gnashing of teeth."

—Matthew 25:14–30 (NIV)

Such a powerful parable! The master gave each according to their present ability. That tells me that the servant who received the five talents had the ability to manage that much responsibility, and the servant who was given two talents had the ability to manage that level of responsibility. The servant who had received one talent was experiencing his first day on the job; he had no track record with the master. We know in the story that the servant who received the five talents went to work right away and made five more, meaning he then had ten talents. The one who received two talents went to work right away and made two talents, bringing his total to four.

You need to understand that when the servant who was given five talents was operating at his current level of responsibility, the master knew that in no way was he operating at his total potential. The five-talent man, at the end of his assignment, then holding ten talents, was a changed man. His capacity had been stretched; he was now a ten-talent man. His capacity to handle responsibility had increased to a higher level than it was when the assignments were handed out. The same was true of the servant who had received the two talents; he had grown it to four talents. Now, let's take a look at the servant who was given one talent:

> Then the man who had received one bag of gold came. "Master," he said, **"I knew that you are a hard man, harvesting where you have not sown and gathering where you have not scattered seed.** So I was afraid and went out and hid your gold in the

ground. See, here is what belongs to you."

His master replied, "You wicked, lazy servant! So you knew that I harvest where I have not sown and gather where I have not scattered seed? Well then, you should have put my money on deposit with the bankers, so that when I returned, I would have received it back with interest. So take the bag of gold from him and give it to the one who has ten bags."

—Matthew 25:24–28 (NIV)

This first-time-out servant had the wrong perspective of the master. He thought he was a hard man. The servant thought that if he went out and spent the talent he was given on seed, and went to the trouble of actually harvesting from that seed, the master would come and take all of it for himself. So, in his mind, he was thinking, "What is in it for me? Nothing!" The servant tried to sound like he had some integrity by declaring he was afraid of losing the talent and then burying it on behalf of protecting it for the master. The master called his bluff, stating, "Well, if you were really concerned for me, you would have at least put it on deposit with the bankers so I would have at least received interest on my money." No, he was not concerned about the master. He was concerned about all the work it would take to raise that crop, which would not profit him at all, which was a wrong assumption. My question is: who told him the master was untrustworthy? Someone did. Here's the part that I really want to point out to you:

So take the bag of gold from him and give it to the one who has ten bags.

—Matthew 25:24–28 (NIV)

In our world of social justice, this statement just does not make sense. Why take it from him and give it to the one who already has ten? Shouldn't he give it to the one who has four? He did a great job and doubled his return, as well as the one who then had ten. But no, the master gave the talent to the one who had ten, who then had eleven. Why?

Because God is after profit. He is consumed with getting a harvest on His investment. He knows that the one who had ten would get the job done! He had been tested previously; this was not his first rodeo, as they say. No, the master had worked with this guy before and had confidence in him.

Let me explain it this way: if you have kids, and you have a job that must get done, you know which one to give the assignment to—the one who will get it done. Well, that is how God is.

Who is God going to give the great business idea to that can be used to bring in millions into the Kingdom or to fund His agenda? The one who will get it done, that's who.

God looked at all of Israel and could not find a widow who would sow her last meal to the prophet. He had to look outside of Israel to find that person. The point is that God is looking over the earth and among His children to see who is ready, who has not quit, and who has stayed strong in the hard places of discipline.

For Drenda and me, overcoming our debt was not a two-week project. It was twenty years of allowing God to mentor and posture us for our future. We launched our own company, stepped out of debt, prospered at a level that I could have only dreamt about just a few years before, and have given millions away to ministry projects over the years. Drenda was able to have her dream house that she designed herself. When we launched the church, it was full of clients and friends who had seen our transformation and wanted to follow us.

My father was not a Christian all these years, but something caught his attention. I could not talk to him about the Lord, as he was always so cynical that I could not even bring the topic up. I would pray and ask God to send someone else to reach him, as I tried and just couldn't. But one day, he just showed up at the church. I heard someone he knew ask him why he showed up, and he said, "I have seen too many things I cannot explain." My dad was born again because, secretly, he was watching our TV broadcast, and he had just seen too many stories of the Kingdom that he couldn't help but believe.

My dad was eighty years old when he gave his heart to God. One of the stories that caught his attention was seeing my daughter's healing of a thirteen-pound tumor. It disappeared overnight as she slept. She had no surgery or medical treatment. God just healed her as she slept after we had prayed for her. He also saw his daughter-in-law with a huge tumor in her abdomen. The doctors gave her four months to live. Yet, like my daughter, her tumor also disappeared as she slept. These public stories and our success drew the discouraged, those in distress, and those in debt to us because of our public victories. Now, by submitting themselves to God's Word, they have their own incredible stories.

The public battle brings your team together. Like David's men in the cave, they found him; he did not recruit them. They made him their leader. It was not a title; it was who David was and what David did that persuaded those who followed. Moses demonstrated publicly that he had heard God, and the people followed him into a new life.

Joseph demonstrated that he heard God when he interpreted the dreams in prison. That drew him to Pharaoh, who had a problem that he could not solve. Thankfully, Pharaoh had heard of Joseph, the one who could hear God. And in so doing, not only was Egypt saved, but so was Israel. Although Pharaoh was in charge, he followed Joseph's lead and told his team to do everything that Joseph said. By following Joseph, Egypt was not only saved from destruction from the horrible famine, but also greatly prospered.

> *There was no food, however, in the whole region because the famine was severe; both Egypt and Canaan wasted away because of the famine. Joseph collected **all the money that was to be found in***

Egypt and Canaan in payment for the grain *they were buying, and he brought it to Pharaoh's palace. When the money of the people of Egypt and Canaan was gone, all Egypt came to Joseph and said, "Give us food. Why should we die before your eyes? Our money is all gone."*

"Then bring your livestock," said Joseph. "I will sell you food in exchange for your livestock, since your money is gone." ***So they brought their livestock to Joseph, and he gave them food in exchange for their horses, their sheep and goats, their cattle and donkeys.*** *And he brought them through that year with food in exchange for all their livestock.*

When that year was over, they came to him the following year and said, "We cannot hide from our lord the fact that since our money is gone and our livestock belongs to you, there is nothing left for our lord except our bodies and our land. Why should we perish before your eyes—we and our land as well? Buy us and our land in exchange for food, and we with our land will be in bondage to Pharaoh. Give us seed so that we may live and not die, and that the land may not become desolate."

So Joseph bought all the land in Egypt for Pharaoh. The Egyptians, one and all, sold their fields, because the famine was too severe for them.

—Genesis 47:13 – 20b (NIV)

When I read this, I always think, I want to hire someone like Joseph with a plan that can change a tragedy into a story. One who could produce a plan like that, which could capture such wealth, is incredible. As you are looking around, thinking that there is no one like that, you are wrong, because you and I are that person. With the Holy Spirit in us, we have God's wisdom, the same wisdom that Joseph had. Again, when we read Joseph's amazing story, let's just remember the journey that brought him there.

We have already covered a lot, but there is still one more battle that you must win to actually occupy your destiny. I call it "the battle to occupy."

CHAPTER NINE

THE BATTLE TO OCCUPY

The third battle that you must win is the battle for occupation: to hold territory for the Kingdom of God. Let me put this battle into perspective. You have already gone through the preparation training, you have won the private battle, you have won the public battle, and people are now drawn to your anointing and your mission. They are now part of your team. Everything is set for you to step into your promise. I know that sounds like fun, and it is, but there is a lot going on at this point. Let me give you an illustration of what I am talking about.

Let's say that you desire to grow something, to be a farmer and raise something. So, you buy some land. You own it, you have taken legal jurisdiction of it, but unless you do something with it, you are not occupying it, you just own it. And if you do nothing with it, weeds and briars will take over the place. Yes, you could say that it was your destiny to own that land, that the land was the place that God was moving you toward all along, but if you do not occupy it, nothing is going to happen. There will be no benefit of owning the land at all.

Remember, our definition of destiny is a place that God has called you to **rule over, or occupy** and control on behalf of His Kingdom.

Let me give you another example from my life. The night that I stood there in that radio station on the first night of our church, and saw the exact picture that God gave me when He called me to preach twenty-one years earlier, was very much stepping into my destiny. And although I technically reached the exact place that God was calling me toward, that does not represent the total definition of what my destiny is. You could say that I am in the door, and that, quite frankly, is awesome! However, there lay before me some serious work that needed to be done, much of it totally new to me.

Occupation leans more toward administration and delegated authority than just owning something in title only. Being able to control and exercise authority over something will require people, thus, the importance of the team you bring with you. Being able to structure your team in order to bring your entire vision to pass will require a complete understanding by your team of how delegated authority works. Your main role is now to administrate the occupation. You will maintain the lead, but you will primarily be the visionary leader. Your success will not be based on how much you can do but on how much you, as a team, can do. You will use a system of delegated assignments and delegated authority to get things done.

You started learning a lot about leading a team ever since people started following you after your public victories, but things will get a lot more intense now. The danger is that you have been in charge for so long that you may feel that you have to know every detail and approve every action at the smallest level. You will need to watch out for that, because you have a team now. You are not capable of doing everything on your own, and if you try, you will become the skinny neck of the funnel. You are not able to occupy the vision that God has given you on your own; that is why the team is there.

Occupation, translated into layman's terms, means people.

We had to have people. It could not just be Drenda and me by ourselves anymore. We had to have a team, and we had to know how to manage the occupation through that team. There were org charts to write, processes to write up, and departments to form. I want to admit something here that may surprise you: I had never seen an org chart up to this point in my life. Yes, I owned and ran a multimillion-dollar company, but it was a company full of commissioned salespeople. I had to run payroll for them, but, quite frankly, they ran

OCCUPATION, TRANSLATED INTO LAYMAN'S TERMS, MEANS PEOPLE.

themselves. If they did not work, they did not make money. I had rules and contracts that they had to sign, and we had training covering what to do and what not to do as far as working with a client went. But we did not have an HR department. They were all 1099 commissioned salespeople. We offered the administration piece of their puzzle, but they were all self-motivated and knew how to sell.

But running a church is not like having a team of self-motivated commissioned salespeople. We had to have an HR department. There were all kinds of labor laws to follow, we had to withhold taxes, and we had to have processes and administration. We had to hire and sometimes fire. There were expenses to be paid and equipment to be purchased. Of course, you start out slowly and move forward as you can, but starting a church was all new to me. Thank God the people who came around us were all excited to follow us, even if we did not feel so confident. At every step, though, God was there.

I think the best picture I can show you of destiny is found in the life of Joshua. Joshua was Moses's right-hand man. He was brave and one of the two spies who actually made it into the promised land because he believed God. In Numbers chapter 14, we find the sad story of the spies coming back from spying out the land with an evil report.

> *The land we explored devours those living in it. All the people we saw there are of great size. We seemed like grasshoppers in our own eyes and we looked the same to them.*

—Numbers 13:32–33 (NIV)

Listen to what Joshua said back to them.

> *Joshua son of Nun and Caleb son of Jephunneh, who were among those who had explored the land, tore their clothes and said to the entire Israelite assembly, "The land we passed through and explored is exceedingly good. If the Lord is pleased with us, he will lead us into that land, a land flowing with milk and honey, and will give it to us. Only do not rebel against the Lord. And **do not be afraid of the people of the land, because we will devour them. Their protection is gone, but the Lord is with us. Do not be afraid of them.***

—Numbers 14:6–9 (NIV)

Joshua was not afraid of them, and he was ready to go. Joshua was a warrior and helped Moses defeat the Amalekites earlier. If that was so, and it is, then why did God spend so much time in the first chapter of Joshua telling him not to be afraid? Good question. Let's find out.

> *No one will be able to stand against you all the days of your life. As I was with Moses, so I will be with you; I will never leave you nor forsake you. Be strong and courageous, because you will lead these people to inherit the land I swore to their ancestors to give them.*

*"**Be strong and very courageous.** Be careful to obey all the law my servant Moses gave you; do not turn from it to the right or to the left, that you may be successful wherever you go. Keep this Book of the Law always on your lips; meditate on it day and night, so that you may be careful to do everything written in it. Then you will be prosperous and successful. **Have I not commanded you? Be strong and courageous. Do not be afraid; do not be discouraged, for the Lord your God will be with you wherever you go.**"*

—Joshua 1:5–9 (NIV)

What was going on? Was Joshua not afraid of the enemy? If we take a closer look, we can see what was going on.

*Be strong and courageous, **because you will lead these people** to inherit the land I swore to their ancestors to give them.*

—Joshua 1:6 (NIV)

It was not the enemy on the other side of the Jordan River that God was encouraging Joshua to face with courage. It was leading the two million people that had caused Moses so much trouble that was the issue.

Before Moses died, God called both him and Joshua to a conference discussing this very issue.

The Lord said to Moses, "Now the day of your death

is near. Call Joshua and present yourselves at the tent of meeting, where I will commission him." So Moses and Joshua came and presented themselves at the tent of meeting.

Then the Lord appeared at the tent in a pillar of cloud, and the cloud stood over the entrance to the tent. And the Lord said to Moses: "You are going to rest with your ancestors, and these people will soon prostitute themselves to the foreign gods of the land they are entering. They will forsake me and break the covenant I made with them. And in that day I will become angry with them and forsake them; I will hide my face from them, and they will be destroyed. Many disasters and calamities will come on them, and in that day they will ask, 'Have not these disasters come on us because our God is not with us?' And I will certainly hide my face in that day because of all their wickedness in turning to other gods.
—Deuteronomy 31:14–18 (NIV)

Oh my gosh! God was commissioning Joshua to lead these people with this kind of pep talk???!!! I am sure that Joshua was standing there in shock. This is why God said three times in a row to Joshua to be courageous. He did not just tell him to have courage. He commanded him to be courageous.

Wow. If God commands you to have courage, you know for sure you are going to need it. God knew that Joshua would be leading the people against walled cities and fierce giants. But the bigger issue was the people that he would be required to lead, not the enemy on the other side of the Jordan. Joshua would be required to deal with conflict in front of him as he faced the enemy nations. He would also be required to deal with conflict on the rear, as he faced the rebellion of the people he was leading.

If Joshua thought he missed what Moses was saying, Moses made it very clear in Deuteronomy 31:27.

> *For I know how rebellious and stiff-necked you are. If you have been rebellious against the Lord while I am still alive and with you, how much more will you rebel after I die!*
>
> — Deuteronomy 31:27 (NIV)

Joshua was there the whole time with Moses and the people in the wilderness. He saw how the people were easily led into sin and rebellion. But more importantly, he also saw how all this grieved and affected Moses.

Here is the deception: people think once they get to their destiny, the place that God has called them to occupy on behalf of the Kingdom, things will be easy, and it will be coasting from that point on. I am sorry to disappoint you, but it is just the opposite. The reason God has to make sure you are spiritually prepared to take your destiny is because there will be problems with people, with the devil, and many other problems that will arise in occupying that territory. Yes, once you get all the weeds cleared out and get the right people in the right places, it does smooth out a bit. There will be trouble, but don't worry. You are anointed for trouble. And God has promised to never leave you.

GOD HAS NOT FORSAKEN ME, AND HE WILL NOT FORSAKE YOU EITHER.

Let me paraphrase what I am saying: Israel came to the promised land, they crossed the Jordan River, but then they had to fight to occupy it. On the front end of reaching your destiny, there may be turmoil as you will have to occupy that destiny. This includes putting the processes and procedures in place to exercise authority over your destiny.

Oh, by the way. Remember your staff!

I can remember when God called me to Tulsa to go to school, and how scary that was. I can remember when God called me into the financial field and living on commissions, how scared I was, and how I hated making those phone calls. I learned to deal with problems there, with reps and clients. I can remember one sales meeting where one of my regional vice presidents stood up and said, "Why should we follow you, Gary? I don't believe you can make any of us successful." This guy was trying to make it without making his phone calls and was in a financial mess. Not my fault. I had trained him how to make the calls. It seemed I was always dealing with attitudes and complaints. Stress was constant. Drenda had to lay her hands on me at night to help me sleep, as fear would try to overtake me.

I can remember when God called me to start the church, how unprepared and scared I felt not knowing how to be a pastor. I can remember when God called us to build the 6.5-million-dollar Now Center when we only had $70,000 in the bank. When we launched our TV programs, we did not have any money in the bank for that project at all, either.

DESTINY CAN BE CHAOS, BUT IT IS THE MOST REWARDING CHAOS THAT YOU WILL HAVE.

But I also remember God being faithful in every situation. I also remember the blessings He has given me and the great life it is to serve Him. God has not forsaken me, and He will not forsake you either.

You will be called by God to love people. They will need to be mentored and trained, but they will grow and mature. On the other hand, they will many times be your biggest problem, and you must know how to handle them.

Destiny can be chaos, but it is the most rewarding chaos that you will have. My mentor always said, "Gary, it is going to get worse. You just have to get better."

CHAPTER TEN

PEOPLE: YOUR ANSWER OR YOUR PROBLEM

Most of the time, when we talk about being in conflict with the devil or demons, we are usually talking about dealing with the devil's people. A demon does not usually want to show itself, as it knows that once you realize it is there, you will deal with it. No, our biggest struggle in occupying the territory that God gives us to occupy is dealing with demon-inspired people, putting the wrong people in the wrong box of responsibility, or hiring incompetent people.

You will need people where you are headed. I have to say, most of the problems, and, quite frankly, the biggest problems, I have had in my ministry and business have been people-related. Then again, the biggest victories I have had in ministry and business have been because of people as well. So, who are you going to put in that box in the organizational chart when you need a job done? Who has

YOU WILL NEED PEOPLE WHERE YOU ARE HEADED.

the character and the ability to occupy that space? It's a big question and one you need to get right. And I will admit, it is hard, but if we follow some good, sound principles of discernment, we can do pretty well.

The first and most important quality to look for, in my opinion, for anyone you put in a place of delegated authority, is that they **<u>MUST</u>** understand how a kingdom works! They must understand how authority flows down from the head of the organization, who they report to, and who reports to them. They must have passed the submission test long ago and must have proven loyalty. Satan is going to try to break the chain of command, and he will look for the weakest link in your structure. Remember, authority flows from the head down, and power follows authority. Satan is going to try to insert himself into your org chart, and yes, there will be a name attached to it. His goal is to stop the flow of power that is intersecting his kingdom here on Earth. And he is going to try to deceive people out of their positions or lure people into positions that are not theirs to take.

You must be sure that when someone down line speaks, they are speaking your words, not theirs. For instance, when I was a young pastor, if I sent someone to the hospital to pray for a person, I would often hear a complaint from the one I sent. They would say the person they were praying for would say, "Well, I thought Pastor Gary was coming." But what they did not understand is that I was there. I was there! See, we have not taught our people about delegated authority. They would say, "No. I want Pastor Gary to come and pray for me." As I told you, I was there. I gave that person my authority when I laid my hands on them and set them in position. They were operating under my authority, my anointing, and the same grace I function under in my assignment. Jesus said, "If you've seen me, you've seen the Father." Exactly! If I send someone in my name, they should say the same thing I would have spoken if I were there. But I wasn't teaching my people that. We've not been taught that, especially in our American culture, have we? Instead, my people would say, "I am sorry, but Pastor Gary could not come to see you today, but I am here to pray for you." No, that makes it sound like I did not care about them. You must train your people that they represent you in any position they are in.

When we were a smaller church, and I had not taught the people how a kingdom works, I heard this kind of comment quite often, "Pastor Gary needs to do this or do that." After I taught my church the truth and instructed them on how a kingdom works and how authority flows down from the head, most of that stopped. The issue in our churches is the spectator style of Christianity we were taught growing up.

I grew up in a denominational church that had a pastor and a secretary who volunteered during the week. That was all. That was it. The pastor did everything. It was his responsibility to do all the weddings, all the funerals, go to the hospital, pray for the sick, and the list went on and on. I can remember hearing my dad complaining about the pastor not visiting someone. He would say, "The pastor should have visited that person, that is why we pay a pastor." That is what people have been taught and what they have seen as an example as the pastor's job. We were never taught that we, the normal, everyday church member, had authority to do the works of Jesus.

When Paul was teaching Pastor Timothy, who pastored the church in Ephesus, how to pick leaders, he said to look at the person's home life. If you look at a person's home life, it will tell you a lot about what that person will duplicate in your organization. I have a friend who is a pastor of a large church, and when he started out, he needed to hire a few people. So, he did the typical thing people do when looking for an employee. He gathered up some resumes, talked to those who applied, and made hires. Sadly, the people he hired did not work out. It seemed that what was written on their resume did not match the level of excellence that he wanted, so he let them go and tried again with the same result. Again, he had to let them go. After analyzing what went wrong, he realized there was a flaw in his hiring procedure: the resume was not telling the whole story, and neither was the applicant.

So, he changed how he interviewed his candidates. After the resume review, which almost meant nothing, he found out, he would ask the candidate to walk him to their car in the parking lot. He wanted to see how well-kept and clean the car was. If there were french fries smashed into the carpet, empty Coke bottles, and trash all through the car, then he knew if he hired that person, his church would end up looking like their car. He even went a step further in his investigation. He would stop by their home, unannounced, in the evening. Same thing. If all the wallpaper was falling off the walls and there was trash all around the house, again, he knew what his church would look like if they were hired. He said that after he started to hire based on this method, he found the people of excellence he was looking for. But the most important thing he looked at was how the family functioned.

Paul told Timothy the most important thing to observe in a candidate was not just a clean car or house but to look for respect and honor in the family. Paul knew that the family was a mini organizational chart. If the father could not properly exercise authority and training there, he knew that there was no way he would have the ability to manage a larger organization like the church.

Today, people are all caught up with titles. But having a title does not make a person qualified for a place of authority! I have made mistakes by putting the wrong people in positions too many times. In the end, it always costs me money and lost time. I remember when we needed to hire a person to work in our TV department. We put out ads with the job description we were hiring for, along with the qualifications needed to accomplish the job. A woman answered the ad and came to us with a great resume. She had worked for a large ministry in a high management position running their TV department and had just left, she said, because the ministry was downsizing its staff. Well, it did not take long before

I became suspicious. She did not know what she was doing at all! I found out through some digging that she never actually worked in a TV department but had only been a writer. And no, the company did not downsize, they had fired her. So, when you are looking for someone to fill a spot in your occupation team, remind yourself to look past the flattery and the great talent. Look at their track record in regard to loyalty and submission.

In First Corinthians, chapter three, Paul was teaching the church in Corinth on this same topic, and he said the following:

> *Brothers and sisters, I could not address you as people who live by the Spirit but as people who are still worldly—mere infants in Christ. I gave you milk, not solid food, for you were not yet ready for it. Indeed, you are still not ready. You are still worldly. For since there is jealousy and quarreling among you, are you not worldly? Are you not acting like mere humans? For when one says, "I follow Paul," and another, "I follow Apollos," are you not mere human beings? What, after all, is Apollos? And what is Paul? Only servants, through whom you came to believe—as the Lord has assigned to each his task.*

> *I planted the seed, Apollos watered it, but God has been making it grow. So neither the one who plants nor the one who waters is anything, but only God, who makes things grow. The one who plants and*

the one who waters have one purpose, and they will each be rewarded according to their own labor. For we are co-workers in God's service; you are God's field, God's building. By the grace God has given me, I laid a foundation as a wise builder, and someone else is building on it. But each one should build with care. For no one can lay any foundation other than the one already laid, which is Jesus Christ.

—1 Corinthians 3:1–11 (NIV)

In verse one, he said, *"Brothers and sisters, I could not address you as people who live by the Spirit but as people who are still worldly—mere infants in Christ. I gave you milk, not solid food, for you were not yet ready for it. Indeed, you are still not ready"* (1 Corinthians 3:1–2, NIV). What does a baby do with solid food? They spit it out, or they change churches. I wish I were kidding, but I'm just telling you how it is. He went on, "Indeed you are still not ready. You are still worldly. For since there is jealousy and quarreling among you, are you not worldly?" (1 Corinthians 3:3a, NIV). Jealousy and quarreling over what? Position. Visibility. Who's more spiritual than someone else.

Are you not acting like mere humans? For when someone says, "I follow Paul," and another, "I follow Apollos," are you not mere human beings? What, after all, is Apollos and what is Paul? Only servants through whom you came to believe—as the Lord has assigned to each his task. I planted the seed, Apollos watered it, but God has been making it grow.

—1 Corinthians 3:3b–6 (NIV)

What is God interested in? God is interested in growth. And these people are all out of order, all enamored with what

GOD IS INTERESTED IN GROWTH. glitters or gets the most attention. They have lost sight of the plan of God: that each person has their own giftings and assignment, and God has given each of them grace for that assignment. Why? So, everything would grow as each part does its part. Paul knew that if the church operated in order, honoring each other's gifts and callings, things would grow!

> *So, neither the one who plants nor the one who waters is anything, but only God, who makes things grow. The one who plants and the one who waters have one purpose, and they will each be rewarded according to their own labor. For we are co-workers in God's service; you are God's field, God's building. But Paul says, "By the grace God has given me, I laid a foundation as a wise builder."*
>
> —1 Corinthians. 3:7–10b (NIV)

Paul told the church that he was able to work with an excellent ability by God's grace. He recognized that the grace he walked in was for a specific purpose and position and was encouraging those in that church to find their place. See, everyone has grace. Every assignment has God's empowerment with it. And one of the plots the enemy uses against you is to pull you out of that grace. For instance, I am not administrative. If I have to deal with administrative things very long, my brain begins to get tired. But it's amazing. I have people on staff who love administration. They love it, love it, love it. And I think, *That's weird. How can you love administration?* The Bible says He gives people different giftings and assigns people to different tasks. When they are in their gifting, they love it; it actually energizes them. So, here's what the enemy wants to do: he wants to pull you out of your grace.

Now, I can teach all day because I am passionate about the Kingdom. I love teaching the Kingdom. I can teach all day. At the end of the day, I'll be tired, but I'll be enthusiastic. I'll have more energy at the end of the day than I did at the beginning of the day, because I'm in my grace, I am in my gifting. But you know what it feels like when you're outside your grace, right? You need to take a nap! You might have friends who call you and dump all their problems on you, and you know what that feels like, right? You see, they have the grace to raise their own family, but when they try to let you take responsibility for the bills they can't pay or the problems they are dealing with, it pulls you outside of your grace and pulls the energy right out of you.

The enemy loves to draw you out of your grace into what is

called "false responsibility." He wants to drag you into false responsibility that you have no grace for, no empowerment by God for. As people try to give you their responsibility and you try to solve all their problems, you have stepped out of position, you will get worn out, and things will stop growing and working right in your life because you are out of place. Paul was saying here that there is grace for a position, an assignment that God gives you, so stay with that. That is where you will find your strength, passion, and contentment. Paul continues:

> Just as a body, though one, has many parts, but all its many parts form one body, so it is with Christ. For we were all baptized by[a] one Spirit so as to form one body—whether Jews or Gentiles, slave or free—and we were all given the one Spirit to drink. Even so the body is not made up of one part but of many.

> Now if the foot should say, "Because I am not a hand, I do not belong to the body," it would not for that reason stop being part of the body. And if the ear should say, "Because I am not an eye, I do not belong to the body," it would not for that reason stop being part of the body. If the whole body were an eye, where would the sense of hearing be? If the whole body were an ear, where would the sense of smell be? But in fact God has placed the parts in the body, every one of them, just as he wanted them to be. If they were all one part, **where would the body be?** As it is, there are many parts, but one body. The eye cannot say

to the hand, "I don't need you!" And the head cannot say to the feet, "I don't need you!"

—1 Corinthians 12:12–21 (NIV)

Where would the body be?

In a big mess, that's where! Imagine a hand trying to be the eye. You would be totally blind. Imagine if the eye were trying to be a foot, you would not be able to move. You would be blind and disabled! Let me say that again, you would be blind and disabled!

Unfortunately, this is where many pastors and CEOs find their church or business. Nothing grows; everything is in chaos and dysfunction.

> *"The eye cannot say to the hand, 'I don't need you!' And the head cannot say to the feet, 'I don't need you!'"*
>
> –1 Corinthians 12:21, NIV

No, Paul knew that this chaos had to be fixed, or they were going nowhere. The eye must take its created place so that the body can see where it is going, and the foot must take its created place so the body can move forward. See, the church of Corinth was very immature, right? We already know that. Paul said, "I can't even talk to you as spiritual." In other words, they couldn't even receive a revelation of their assignment yet. They couldn't even receive a revelation of their destiny yet. You know why? Because they couldn't see past themselves. They were all fighting over who was more spiritual, who was getting all the attention. They were in strife about who was the greatest preacher, Paul or Apollos. And they missed the entire point. It wasn't about Paul or Apollos. It was about God and things growing. They were out of order! In fact, I do not think they even knew that there was an order. They were spiritual babies. So, when we, the body of Christ, want to self-promote ourselves or refuse to stay submitted to where God has assigned us to function, it brings all kinds of problems.

> *For where you have envy and selfish ambition, there you find **disorder and every evil practice**.*
>
> —James 3:16 (NIV)

I once had a lady back in the beginning of the church come up to me after a morning prayer meeting, red in the face, and angry. In tears, she asked this question, "Why didn't you call on me to pray?" "Was I obligated to call on you to pray?" I asked. "No", she said. I then asked her, "Who's in charge of this meeting? Who has the authority over this meeting? I do."

I didn't tell her she was going to pray. I never even brought it up to her before the meeting that she might be called on to pray. And here she was in tears, "Why didn't you call on me to pray?" So, I said to her, "Because of how you're acting right now, that's why I did not call on you." See, I knew that she wanted to be seen praying among the ladies; it was an identity thing for her. I also knew that her house was out of order. There was strife between her and her husband. I told her, "You need to pray and ask God to show you why you thought it was so important that you prayed today in the meeting." So, was the lady that I just mentioned qualified to be given authority over anything? Absolutely not! She was a baby and an immature person. And as it is with babies, they think they are grown up when they are not.

Now, you can stay in a place of immaturity, or you can choose to grow and stay submitted. I would have liked to say she chose to grow, but she did what the majority of people do when they are coached: she left the church. What she did not understand was that she could change churches, but she would have to pass the same test there.

People who are immature don't realize they're immature.

I believe maturity is not measured by someone's talent or gifting or age, but in their ability to stay submitted when they disagree or are corrected. If you have raised kids, you know that they will beg to do something long before they are mature enough to do it. That is normal with kids, but that is also why they have parents who have wisdom. Now, I'm trying to help you here. I know you want to grow. I know you want to reach your destiny and occupy the place God has ordained you to occupy for Him, but Satan plays on immaturity, and I

PEOPLE WHO ARE IMMATURE DON'T REALIZE THEY'RE IMMATURE.

want to help you avoid his traps, so I need to continue this discussion for a bit longer.

> *Do not let anyone who delights in false humility and the worship of angels **disqualify you**. Such a person also goes into great detail about what they have seen; they are puffed up with idle notions by their unspiritual mind. They have lost connection with the head, from whom the whole body, supported and held together by its ligaments and sinews, grows as God causes it to grow.*
>
> —Colossians 2:18–19 (NIV)

Do not let anyone who delights in false humility and the worship of angels **disqualify you for the prize.**

First of all, let's be clear. There is a prize, a reward when you fulfill your assignment with God. Paul says you want to make sure that someone else does not disqualify you for that prize. Kind of a strange statement, isn't it? How could someone else disqualify you for your prize? Isn't your prize based on what you do, not what someone else does? Yes, but what if you never did what you were supposed to do because this other person makes you feel so inadequate that you never try? They make themselves look so spiritual, and you look at yourself and think, *I'm nothing. I don't have words of knowledge very often. I don't see angels. I don't have dreams every night. Maybe I can't hear God.* So, spiritually, you just give up. You're intimidated by them, view yourself in an inferior light, and they make you feel that you must yield what you felt was your assignment or position to them since they are so capable. Is this making sense? So, in reality, you disqualify yourself because you no longer see yourself as qualified in comparison to them. Paul went on and told us exactly how this happens.

> *Such a person also goes into great detail about what they have seen; they are puffed up with idle notions by their unspiritual mind.*
>
> —Colossians 2:18b (NIV)

Have you ever met a Christian who's always telling you the dream they had last night or how God spoke to them this morning and told them to wear the pink dress instead of the blue one? Their conversations are always about what God showed them, their latest dream, or the amazing time they just had in worship, where God showed them this picture or that picture. And let's say God does, in fact, speak to them at that level and shows them things by the minute. Why do they feel they need to constantly tell you about it? Paul says their minds are filled with idle thoughts. What do those thoughts sound like? *I'm better than you are. I am more spiritual than you are. I should be running that department.* Or, *I could have done a better job teaching that class.* Or, *I can teach better than the pastor. In fact, I should be the pastor of this church.* Here's the deal: guess what? You're not the pastor of the church. That spot is occupied. And yes, you may, in fact, teach better than your pastor, but God has not given you that position to occupy.

Paul went on to say, "[These people] have lost connection with the head" (Colossians 2:19a, NIV).

Okay, stop everything! We have a problem. How does authority flow? From the head down. But now they see themselves as the authority, the head, but, of course, they are not. So, what happens next in the church is that the person goes to other, immature, baby Christians and starts doing what we have just read in 1 Corinthians 3, where they begin to believe puffed-up thoughts of their importance. *I should be the hand. I should be the head. I should be the eye.* Right? You've all heard it. Here's the thing I want you to understand: the eye was already created as an eye before it wanted to be a foot. It was created as an eye! God himself has already created you specifically for Himself with your unique giftings and talents. He has a place for you, and He reveals that to us as our character matures and we are able to receive that promotion without saying, "Hey, look at me!"

GOD HIMSELF HAS ALREADY CREATED YOU SPECIFICALLY FOR HIMSELF WITH YOUR UNIQUE GIFTINGS AND TALENTS.

We need to understand that God will give us assignments. They will start small, but as we are faithful with the little, we will gain credibility with God and men. We will be promoted by those He has put over us, and He will move us into different assignments as we mature. This is how it works, and there are no shortcuts.

Because immaturity and pride hide behind talent and flatter, Paul says you need to test anyone you are considering for leadership. Again, test them for what? Talent? No, their ability to stay submitted. As I have said before, the church is very immature in understanding its role in occupation, which, of course, is what Jesus told us to do. Most of the church is focused on conquering the devil, as I have said. Because of this, people have not matured in their understanding and ability to occupy.

Satan wants to stop the flow of power, tear down authority, and many times, he does it through deception. We must always be on guard to see past what might be on the surface of a situation to understand the hidden motives and tactics that the devil may be setting up underground. For instance, I know we have all seen the blue medical insignia that hospitals and health companies use. It is a picture of a pole with a snake on it.

> *They traveled from Mount Hor along the route to the Red Sea, to go around Edom. But the people grew impatient on the way; they spoke against God and against Moses, and said, "Why have you brought us up out of Egypt to die in the wilderness? There is no bread! There is no water! And we detest this miserable food!"*

> *Then the Lord sent venomous snakes among them; they bit the people and many Israelites died. The people came to Moses and said, "We sinned when we spoke against the Lord and against you. Pray that the Lord will take the snakes away from us." So Moses prayed for the people.*
>
> *The Lord said to Moses, "Make a snake and put it up on a pole; anyone who is bitten can look at it and live." So Moses made a bronze snake and put it up on a pole. Then when anyone was bitten by a snake and looked at the bronze snake, they lived.*
>
> —Numbers 21:4–9 (NIV)

So, one day Drenda was reading this, and the Lord said to her, "Do you think that snake on the pole that Moses put up was alive on that pole?" "Of course not," she said. But then God said, "Take a closer look at what your doctors use as their symbol of medical help against disease and death." God spoke to her, "Is there one snake on that pole?" "No", she said, "there are two." God then said to her, "And are those snakes dead? No! Dead snakes do not curl up a pole. They hang limp."

Wow, I had seen that symbol all my life, and my mind always thought, *That is so great. The medical community recognizes that God is the source of life.* They are using the image God gave Israel to signify that the snake, Satan's jurisdiction over their health, was dead. But now I realize, no, that is not a symbol in agreement with God's jurisdiction over Satan. It is a symbol of defiance! On top of that, it is not one snake, but two! When you start looking, it is interesting how many things you begin to see where Satan has infiltrated society with his perverted lies and arrogance against God and His people.

Satan hijacked and has perverted the rainbow, a promise of God, and he will try to hijack your authority that stands against him. He must break that **chain of authority**. He wants to stop that power from flowing into his domain. How does he do that? Through people, of course. And like the snakes on that pole, it is easy to assume that you know what is going on. But you need to take a second look and trust the Holy Spirit to help you sniff out Satan's plans before they manifest. There are many tactics he will use, more than I could cover here, but let me name a few of the most common strategies he uses to sneak into your occupation team.

THE NUMBER ONE WAY SATAN GAINS ACCESS TO YOUR AUTHORITY IS THROUGH IGNORANCE.

The number one way Satan gains access to your authority is through ignorance.

So many believers are still praying to God to fix their problems. "God, you do something about it. You do something about this sickness. You do something about this poverty. You do something about..." They don't realize that He has already given them the authority to deal with it. This is why I teach so often about the authority and the position God has given us in the Kingdom.

> *Truly I tell you, whatever you **bind** on earth will be bound in heaven, and whatever you loose on earth will be loosed in heaven.*
>
> *—Matthew 18:18 (NIV)*

So, what are you binding? What are you loosing? He's given you the keys to the Kingdom. You have that authority. Use the keys! Sadly, so many people, so many Christians still say things like, "God allows bad things to happen. God kills people." Friend, we are talking about basic 101 Kingdom law here, even below 101. If they do not understand this basic fact of Kingdom life, how would they ever be able to rule over the enemy or carry your delegated authority? No, it's not possible. They will not be able to do it!

> *Consider it pure joy, my brothers and sisters, whenever you face trials of many kinds, because you know that the testing of your faith produces perseverance. Let perseverance finish its work so that you may be mature and complete, not lacking anything. If any of you lacks wisdom, you should ask God, who gives generously to all without finding fault, and it will be given to you. But when you ask, you must believe*

and not doubt, because the one who doubts is like a wave of the sea, blown and tossed by the wind. That person should not expect to receive anything from the Lord. Such a person is double-minded and unstable in all they do.

—James 1:2–8 (NIV)

I love this Scripture because it gives you a great guideline for who you need on your occupation team. Let me go through the three points.

Consider it pure joy, my brothers and sisters, whenever you face trials of many kinds, because you know that the testing of your faith produces perseverance. Let perseverance finish its work so that you may be mature and complete, not lacking anything.

—James 1:2–4 (NIV)

Okay, point number one: They should realize there will be trials in any position of authority. Depending on how high up the authority chain you are going to place them, the more experience they will need in dealing with Satan's tactics. No matter where they are on your occupation hierarchy org chart, they should have some experience with trials and using God's Word to stand their ground when challenged. In a trial, James said that a believer "KNOWS" that the testing of their faith cannot fail. Through perseverance, not quitting, and staying steadfast on the Word, they will be complete and lack NOTHING! The Word never fails. You do not want an immature believer calling you, crying, and wringing their hands in fear, asking how to deal with every little problem that comes along. You want someone who can hold their position in agreement with the Word and with the assignment given to them.

> *If any of you lacks wisdom, you should ask God, who gives generously to all without finding fault, and it will be given to you.*
>
> —James 1:5 (NIV)

Point number two: They need to know that they can go to God for wisdom in how to handle the trial they find themselves in, and He will give it liberally.

> *But when you ask, you must believe and not doubt, because the one who doubts is like a wave of the sea, blown and tossed by the wind. That person should not expect to receive anything from the Lord. Such a person is double-minded and unstable in all they do.*
>
> —James 1:6–8 (NIV)

Lastly, they can't be double-minded. They should EXPECT the Word to work just as God says it will. In contrast, if you put a weak person in a position, one who is weak in faith and untested, this Scripture says they will be unstable in ALL their ways. ALL their ways. If you have a business, are you going to put some employee on the front line who is unstable?

If you were commanding an army, would you give an assignment, a vital assignment where many lives matter, to someone you know is unstable? Someone who does not know how to handle his sword? No, you would not. Unfortunately, it seems so many Christians are just learning how to keep the devil out of their own house. Until they learn how to do that, please do not give them more responsibility. You cannot have wishy-washy people on your team and expect to win. Know what the Word says and then stand on it. "Well, Pastor, I'm still afraid." Well, that's fine. Everyone grows up and learns who they are, but you need to win that battle at home before you can handle a public battle.

Goliath was not David's first day out. I have talked about this. He actually took a bear and a lion on with his bare hands when they threatened the family's sheep. That is some pretty intense stuff! David had evidence that he was a believer in God's word. What he had done in private with no one watching, he then did in the public arena with Goliath. And what that person you are hiring has done or not done in the public arena may be a clue that you are looking for.

God's not going to send you on an assignment to occupy territory on behalf of the Kingdom when you're unstable, wavering back and forth, and untrained. "Well, can I trust God in this situation?" If you have to ask that question, then the answer would be, "No." If you find that you are afraid, you'd better stay put. "But Pastor, I don't like my job." You're staying put. In fact, the more you don't like your job, the better, because you're learning submission with a good heart and you're learning to do things as unto the Lord. Until you

UNTIL YOU PERSEVERE AS UNTO THE LORD, HE CAN'T TRUST YOU.

persevere as unto the Lord, He can't trust you. You must win the private battle before God will put you in the public battle. Amen.

God is protecting not only you, but He's also protecting His name as well.

Whoever can be trusted with very little can also be trusted with much, and whoever is dishonest with very little will also be dishonest with much. So if you have not been trustworthy in handling worldly wealth, who will trust you with true riches? And if you have not been trustworthy with someone else's property, who will give you property of your own?

—Luke 16:10–12 (NIV)

You're in training. You're going to start out in training. "But Gary, I don't like my boss." You've got to change your mindset. If you want to be effective, you must be trained. Can the boss trust you with their company, with their money? Oh, you might say that you are not in charge of any of the boss's money. Yes, you are! If you are not getting your work done or you are wasting time, you are wasting their money. If you understand that you have been given a trust with someone else's property at that job, you will realize that your next promotion is based on how well you do with that responsibility. Your assignment while you are there is not about you, but about your boss, the one who hired you. Can your boss trust you to accomplish what they have assigned you to do?

"But Gary, I really don't like my boss." That's beside the point. Do you think that Joseph liked being a slave to Potiphar? Do you think that Joseph liked being in that prison? Yet he did such a great job that the jailer put him in charge of the entire prison. The Lord is the one who promotes you. He knew where Joseph was in prison. He knew where Moses was out in the wilderness. He knew where David was with the sheep. He knows your name. Don't you think He knows your name? He knows your name. He knows where you're at.

The hard times you may be facing are helping you learn to be faithful. So, whatever you are doing, if you love it or not, do it with your whole heart as unto the Lord, and He will reward you. Secondly, look for people who have taken the same road of faithfulness that you have taken and you will find your occupation team!

I want to talk about a mistake that every leader makes: putting immature people in a place of authority before they are ready.

Brothers and sisters, I could not address you as people who live by the Spirit but as people who are still worldly—mere

THE HARD TIMES YOU MAY BE FACING ARE HELPING YOU LEARN TO BE FAITHFUL.

infants in Christ.

—1 Corinthians 3:1 (NIV)

If you are leading people, you need to realize that Satan will send people, and God will send people. If you have a business, Satan will send people. If you have a church, Satan will send people. And then people will also send themselves your way, desiring to be on your team, and they all may look very talented. They're also almost always very flattering. But I have learned the hard way that I don't care what they say or what their credentials are. They ALL need to be tested first, before you put them into a position. Get some tissues ready as I share some of my worst stories of violating this essential principle. [1]

---

1 Parts of this chapter were taken from my book, *Occupy Your Destiny: The Winning Strategy for Life* book.

PEOPLE: YOUR ANSWER OR YOUR PROBLEM–CONTINUED

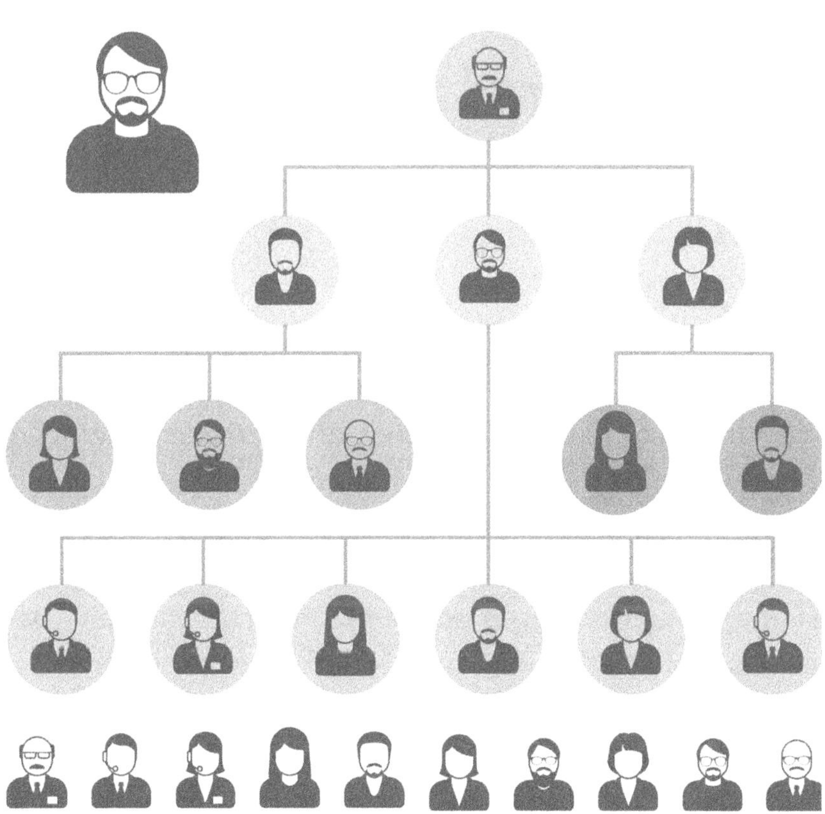

Take a good look at the picture above, because you will need to draw one just like it to occupy the territory that God calls you to. As you can see in this picture, every part, every box, must be faithful to its authority and the fulfillment of the designated assignment for its box. Paul uses an example of the human body to illustrate that every part needs to function for the body to grow.

From him the whole body, joined and held together by **every** *supporting ligament, grows and builds itself up in love, as each* **part** *does its work.*

—Ephesians 4:16 (NIV)

TO BE IN ALIGNMENT WITH THE KING, YOU MUST BE IN ALIGNMENT WITH THE ONE YOU REPORT TO.

Every part working with its unique function provides the complete picture of the King's will; the authority of the Kingdom flowing down into the earth realm.

You're in one of those boxes, or possibly several, but you're part of that puzzle, that complete picture. If one of those boxes fails to perform, tries to change the objective, or is unclear what the king's will is, we have a problem. The entire structure becomes dysfunctional, a dysfunctional organization that is not in alignment with the head. It becomes a dysfunctional org chart. Dysfunctional means it's not functioning. It's useless as far as bringing the will of the king or CEO into reality. It cannot accomplish or finish that task. Now, the point I am making is that every person must be in their assigned place. To be in alignment with the king, you must be in alignment with the one you report to. I did not say you have to like them. I said you have to be in alignment with the instructions they are getting from their leader. There is no other option at play here. The success of the entire organization depends on it. This is why the first thing they teach you in the military is to obey orders.

Ignorance is the basic beginning point of failure. If you don't understand your personal authority, am I going to put you in a place of authority? No. Neither is God. This is why the enemy has tried to convince most of the churches that God does bad things to good people. If you cannot trust Him, you will not follow His direction and will question His motives.

But if people understood that God is good and only good, and His promise means exactly what it says, then people would line up behind that. Then God's power would flow and become dangerous to the enemy. Let me paraphrase what I just said so it applies to the secular realm: if you do not know how your company structure works, where you're at on that org chart, you need to find out. If you are all over the place, talking to anyone and everyone about things outside your area of responsibility, or voicing disagreement with the direction the company is taking, you are overstepping your boundaries. This kind of behavior makes you a dysfunctional and dangerous person on the org chart and to the company as a whole. You may think, *Well, I only talk to people when the boss is not around.* But you know what? God sees all of it.

IGNORANCE IS THE BASIC BEGINNING POINT OF FAILURE.

Everyone wants promotion, but so many do not pay the price to be qualified. Let me illustrate with a story. It's the story of Saul, the first king of Israel. The prophet Samuel had anointed him as king, but now we have a problem. God was telling Samuel to go tell Saul he was now disqualified and could no longer be the king. I think your next question should be, "Why? How did King Saul become disqualified?" Well, the Amalekites were attacking Israel and had set themselves against the Lord. So, God told King Saul to wipe them out. Saul was also instructed not to bring any of the animals back with him from the battle. In verse 13, we see Saul speaking to Samuel after returning from the battle.

Saul speaking to Samuel after returning from the battle.

> *"The Lord bless you! I have carried out the Lord's instructions."*

> *But Samuel said, "What then is this bleating of sheep in my ears? What is this lowing of cattle that I hear?" Saul answered, "The soldiers brought them from the Amalekites; they spared the best of the sheep and cattle to sacrifice to the Lord your God, but we totally destroyed the rest."*

"Enough!" Samuel said to Saul. "Let me tell you what the Lord said to me last night."

"Tell me," Saul replied.

Samuel said, "Although you were once small in your own eyes, did you not become the head of the tribes of Israel? The Lord anointed you king over Israel. And he sent you on a mission, saying, 'Go and completely destroy those wicked people, the Amalekites; wage war against them until you have wiped them out.' Why did you not obey the Lord? Why did you pounce on the plunder and do evil in the eyes of the Lord?"

—1 Samuel 15:13b–19 (NIV)

<u>Verse 20 gives him away. What were first words</u>?

"But I did obey."

—1 Samuel 15:20a (NIV)

Whoa, back up. Samuel repeated exactly what God had said to King Saul, and again, Saul countered it with, "But I did obey." Yet he did not do what God said, did he? To make a long story short, he disqualified himself. God said, "Can't have this." If you want to be qualified for promotion in life, you need to do what those in authority over you ask you to do. Pretty simple, isn't it?

Your kids say, "I cleaned my room." So, you go to check it out, to verify that it is indeed cleaned. You go into their bedroom, and it looks great until you look under the bed. They just threw everything under the bed, right? Threw everything in the closet. No, no, no, no. Nice try, but no, no. We need to show you how to really do this. When you're 50 years old and still throwing stuff under the bed, we have a problem because God can't trust you. And when you're 50 years old, it won't simply be clothes under the bed. It might be not claiming all your income on your tax return or cheating on your wife if we don't get this straightened out.

> *Whoever walks in integrity walks securely, but whoever takes crooked paths will be found out.*
> —Proverbs 10:9 (NIV)

We live in an instant society where everyone is self-promoting themselves and trying to bypass God's promotion system. I was never more shocked to see two young people from our youth department advertising themselves as life coaches. Really! I see all the glamour shots the young ladies are putting on Instagram. Everyone wants to be famous, a movie star. In reality, self-promotion does not work. Even though a person may look perfect on their social media account, when you hire them, you may find that they do not have a clue. And secondly, you do not want to get ahead of your character and your wisdom and self-promote yourself into a disaster.

We were a young church, maybe with 70 people attending,

when on a Wednesday night service, our drummer called in sick. I had this brilliant idea as a young pastor who knew no better, to ask if anyone there played the drums. A young man stepped up and said he did. I asked him if he was a good drummer, and he said yes. I really never knew that he was a drummer, but he had been attending the church for a while, so I said to go ahead. Well, you can imagine what happened. He could not hold a beat if his life depended on it. It got so bad that we had to stop him and have him sit down. Now, of course, he felt humiliated, which was not my intention, but he left me no choice. Well, let me back up. He did give me a choice. I was the mature pastor who brought him up there.

Or take the time that one of my elders came to my office before service and told me that one of the greeters who manned the front door was passing out an invitation to everyone who came through to a picnic that she was hosting the following Sunday, starting at the exact time our service started. I could not believe it! I had to correct that situation in a hurry from the podium. People who have not been taught or tested should never be put in a position of authority, even if it is something as simple as being the greeter! As a leader, you do not want to be surprised by someone's incompetence or their bad attitude after the fact. Without exception, let a man be tested before you place them in a position of authority. Every business owner has found out that a resume doesn't quite tell you the whole story.

I've had people on staff through the years who had side-

YOU CAN'T TRUST PEOPLE WHO PROMOTE THEMSELVES TO CARRY OUT YOUR INSTRUCTIONS.

ministries or side-businesses. Now, I am all for doing things on the side. I usually encourage it as long as they fulfill their obligation to me with excellence. But on more than one occasion, I would find my staff member hanging around our guest speakers with their brochures in hand, talking to them about using their side-hustle company for this and that. I am always shocked by people's lack of common sense and lack of integrity. More than once, I found my vendors had hired out my staff after hours to work on their projects while my projects were late. So many people are hirelings. They are with you as long as there are no better offers somewhere else. You can't trust people who promote themselves to carry out your instructions.

Over the years, I have had employees who work in the computer department, let's say, and it is like pulling teeth to get things done well and on time. But I would go online to their Facebook page or their websites because they have this little side business, and I would be so shocked to find their website laid out so perfectly, so vibrant, with illustrations and pictures. And every link **works**! (I think all you leaders know why I bolded and underlined **works.**) As I scroll through their page, I am impressed with the excellence they portray, but many times I find no mention of any event at church, ever. How can you work full-time somewhere as exciting as a church without saying anything about the men's meeting, the breakfast, or the VBS?

This tells you where they are at, right?

People who self-promote themselves will always choose themselves in a decision. They will always choose themselves in a decision because they'll always put themselves first. They're always subconsciously looking for a better-paying job and view every place they work as a stepping stone to their next opportunity. Now, if you ask them if that was true, they'd say no. But subconsciously, they're always looking. They're always open. They're always kind of "this is temporary" in their mindset. You might say, "Well, Pastor Gary, what's wrong with that?" Well, I don't believe the church operates as the world does.

Here's what I mean by that. When God called Drenda and me to launch Faith Life Church, we didn't have a list of options if this didn't work out. God said, "Launch a church." We knew it was going to cost us something. We did not launch the church to make money. We launched the church because God said to. We covered much of the expense, paid a lot of the payroll, and emptied our bank accounts more than once. We did not take a salary for years after the church started, but instead earned our own money from our business.

Now, I believe my staff members should feel called here. I do not mean they need to come here thinking they will be here forever. But they need to know that God has led them here. If God tells you that you're to be someplace, you can put the resumes away because you know you are where you are supposed to be. God will tell you when it's

"WHEN GOD SPEAKS, STAY THERE UNTIL HE SPEAKS AGAIN."

time to investigate another option. But if you come in on day one searching Google for a better job that same night, we have a problem. Now, there are positions in every organization that are designed to be temporary. I am not talking about those types of positions. Listen, God knows where you are at, He knows your name. You don't have to be second-guessing every move you make. Before I was married, I attended a church in Tulsa for a couple of years. I cannot remember anything my pastor said back then except one message. I'll never forget this phrase, "When God speaks, stay there until He speaks again." That one message has held me so many times when I have wanted to run, hide, or quit.

Slaves (employees) obey your earthly masters with respect and fear and with sincerity of heart, just as you would obey Christ. Obey them not only to win their favor when their eye is on you, but as slaves of Christ, doing the will of God from your heart. Serve wholeheartedly, as if you were serving the Lord, not people, because you know the Lord will reward each one for whatever good they do, whether they are slave or free.

—Ephesians 6:5–8 (NIV)

Joseph didn't market himself on Facebook out of prison, right? God brought him out, and God will move you, too. He knows the plans He has for you more than you even want great plans for yourself. He knows exactly what you're being mentored for.

You do not know what you don't know. God knows where you're headed. And that place you may despise working at now is part of your mentoring needed to someday be somewhere else. "But Gary, I already told you I hate my job." That's good. That means you must choose to submit, not that you want to submit. You need that. You need to choose to submit because that is how authority operates. Yes, you'll not be there that long. If you submit to that job with a willing heart and you're the best on the team, guaranteed, God will move you on. He'll show you the next step. Now, if you want to stay there forever, just keep mumbling and complaining about how you hate going to work and all that. You'll be there a while or in a different place like that one.

I went to college and came out with an Old Testament major. When I got out, God did not tell me what I would be doing. I wasn't called to pastor then. He just said, "You're going to preach my Word."

When I got out of school, I thought, "What's next?" Well, as I told you before, He led me into finances. I was shocked! Into finances! I knew I was called to preach, but what was going on? I had to trust Him for the next step. I was not going to market myself someplace I did not belong.

Anyway, if you remember, Paul talked about self-promotion in chapter 3 of First Corinthians. That church in Corinth was all about self-promotion, because they were babies.

These are baby Christians. Babies cannot be promoted into a place of authority. Babies think they're mature when they're babies. Babies think because they have giftings by the Holy Spirit, they're mature enough to walk into a place of responsibility.

Does anybody have kids who want to drive at age nine? They're not ready for that. You need to be mentored and grow and mature from being a baby to a person who can handle responsibility.

NOTHING GOOD COMES OUT OF DISORDER.

James 3:16a (NIV) says, *"Where you have envy and selfish ambition, there you'll find…"* what? Everyone is out of order, and the org chart is in a big fighting mess. In fact, one version says, there's *"confusion and every evil work"* (James 3:16b, NIV). There's no flow of authority. Everyone's out for themselves. Everyone thinks they have a better idea. Everyone thinks they should be the boss. Kind of sounds like the country, doesn't it? Kind of. Anyway, it gets into a big mess, and it is a big mess. Nothing good comes out of disorder.

You will not be able to occupy anything in that mess. God's power can't flow down through that mess.

I remember talking to a pastor of a large church who said he was having all kinds of problems. So, he brought in a new COO to help him. I was with that COO when I talked to this pastor, and he said, "The first thing I did was fire about one third of the staff and redesign the org chart. I looked for people who wanted to be there, who went the extra mile and smiled while they did it." Well, that pastor's church took off. In five years, it grew to six times the size it had been and became a worldwide ministry.

You need to deal with the chaos and put order into your org chart. Remember, babies are all about me, me, me. That is ok when they are young in the Lord, and they are growing. But you certainly would never put a baby in a place of authority; they usually do not even know what authority is at that point. They just want their milk and to be put to bed.

Another way the enemy comes in to steal your future and get you out of order is by luring you into taking false responsibility. False responsibility is trying to fix something without having the authority to fix it.

Have you ever done that? Cost you a lot of money, didn't it? Yeah. Taking on someone else's responsibility... I have endless stories like that, and I've done it myself. I think we've all done that.

One family, years ago, was losing their house, and they told everyone about it. Now, typically, you would think that people would not want to share that they're losing their house. In church, that's a good place to do it because someone may want to help you out. I'm not against generosity. Please understand me. But the problem was that this person didn't have a job. I talked to him about that. I said, "Why don't you have a job? Your house is going into foreclosure?" "Well, I'm waiting for this other job to open up." I said, "Well, you can get a job while you are waiting for that dream job to open someday. I'll even help you find—" "No, no, I don't want those jobs. I'm believing for this certain job." I thought, "Are you kidding me? You're going to let your family starve and lose your house? There is provision on the way to your promise. I mean, come on. You've got to feed the family while you're looking and waiting for that job." A family in the church gave him the $10,000, and he got the house caught up, but they lost the house in three months anyway. It was foreclosed on, still waiting for that job. Sorry, that is just plain ignorance.

"Well, Pastor, aren't we to be generous?" Yes, but it has to be met with responsibility. When people come to Faith Life Church and say, "Hey, I can't pay my bills," we have a plan and a process to help them. We don't take on the responsibility of paying their bills. We'll help them this month and maybe two at the most, but during that time, we put them in a training system of financial management.

We work with them, helping them get stable, but we do not

pay their bills. You have to meet us halfway. You've got to do your part. We're not the piggy bank. You are the one who is responsible for the issues, and you will have to admit that and take ownership. God will help you. I meet so many grandmas who are broke because they're paying all their kids' bills. Stop it, Grandma. Stop it. "Well, they'll starve to death." Well, I guarantee, they won't starve to death. They may starve a little bit, but that's a good starve. If they get hungry enough, they will work it out. Taking false responsibility for someone else does not allow them to grow up.

As I said previously, when we started our church, I had never seen an org chart because I was in sales. I never hired people as employees until we started the church. As it grew, I knew I needed some help, so I hired a few employees. But I found out very quickly that managing sales reps and managing employees were two different things altogether. We would have weekly staff meetings, and here is how they usually went: "Pastor, we have a big church picnic coming up, as you know. Do you want hot dogs or hamburgers?" Or, "Should we provide ketchup, mustard? How about mayonnaise? What do you want there? Paper plates or plastic plates? What color do you want them to be? Do you want us to email that information out to the church, or do you want

TAKING FALSE RESPONSIBLIITY FOR SOMEONE ELSE DOES NOT ALLOW THEM TO GROW UP.

to announce it from the podium? How about hot chocolate? Should we have that?"

Now multiply those questions by five, seven, or ten employees, and it will drive you nuts. But I didn't know any better; this was all new to me. No one ever taught me how this works. I thought it was my responsibility to have all the answers and to make all the decisions. You can guess what happened. I began to despise my position. I was micromanaged into complete dysfunction. I told Drenda one day, "I'm resigning. I love my company, and I love God, but I don't like pastoring a church. It's just not working."

We had a pastor come through the church as a guest speaker, and we were talking with him about all the dysfunctions we were dealing with. Then he said something that totally changed my perspective on things. He said, "Gary, you don't owe your church the responsibility to fix all their personal problems. All you owe them is to be an example and to have fun."

I understood the example part. I have the example. My marriage was great, we were out of debt, and we had seen God do mighty things. So, I understood being an example. But did you say fun? That kind of threw me. I said, "You said fun, didn't you?" He said, "Yes." Fun. Are you kidding? Fun?

I mean, I have everyone's problems. I'm thinking about everyone's problems. I'm taking false responsibility for their marriages and for their bills. I'm thinking of their kids. I'm thinking all of this stuff, right? I told him that I wouldn't wish this chaos on my worst enemy, let alone be an inspiration to others who want to follow in the ministry.

Friend, that's not how it works. I had no idea how to occupy for God. But I have a great wife who wanted to help me find out how. Drenda found a gentleman who helps pastors and leaders learn how to lead, how to occupy for God. His name is Dean Radtke, and he works with leaders all over the world.

We found a conference he was speaking at, and we went. When I met Dean Radtke, he talked about all the pastors and leaders who are quitting every day because Bible schools don't teach you how to pastor, with administration, legal issues, HR departments, health insurance, and tax issues, all that stuff. They didn't teach you that. The same goes for business owners who have a great idea and jump into it, and start drowning in the details.

At his conference, he had three big whiteboards up front, and he filled each one of them up. I'm like, "Okay. This is really intense here." I really did not understand half of what he was saying, but I knew beneath all the data was the answer I needed. Drenda lined up for me and her to sit down with him three days, nonstop, from 9:00 a.m. to 10:00 p.m. Yes, those were three intense days. He went through all those charts, just very slowly, over and over.

One thing caught my attention. He said, "Gary, it's going to get worse. You will need to get better." That's when I said, "I'm almost done with you," but he was right. You must get better. You must learn how that authority flows, who's responsible.

He said, "Stay in the box." He pointed to that org chart he had drawn on the big white board and said, "Gary, you've got to stay in the box. You're the leader. You don't want to jump down here four layers deep and help them stuff boxes for the weekend service. You're the head. You give instruction and direction."

In fact, here's what he said my job was: "This is the job of anyone who is leading a team of people. You provide direction and expectation. You obtain plans, ideas, and recommendations from your team. You then approve a plan and then commission the work. You then provide the tools necessary to ensure success. Then you obtain an evaluation to further tweak the plan later." He pulled up a picture of an org chart and said, "Teach your people to stay in their box. If their name is in the box, they have it. If their name's in the box, they're responsible. They don't need to be hopping over to someone else's box, they have their own box that they're responsible for. To be effective, your people need to know what box they are reporting to above them on the chart, what boxes are under their responsibility, and who is reporting to them. That is all they really need to focus on."

It was so important to learn that. For those of you who understand an org chart and have been trained in corporate

America, you are probably laughing, but seriously, I had no idea. Here is the mistake I was making. I was hiring people who needed help instead of hiring people who could help me. I was hiring people who did not know much more than I did, instead of people who knew a lot of things I did not know that I needed to know. I needed people with strengths and knowledge that I didn't have. It was definitely a change for me, but learning how an org chart works completely changed my life.

Our ministry grew to become a worldwide ministry in more than sixty nations and on daily TV in every time zone in the world. Thousands of people have had their lives changed because Drenda and I–just two people who did not quit. Yes, Dean Radtke was right, it was going to get worse, and I had to get better. He was so right. I just needed a little coaching on how the org chart works, how authority flows down through the boxes with precision and accountability.

Another way Satan likes to disrupt the flow of authority is through what I call "hijacking authority." Let's go back to our story regarding King Saul being disqualified. After Saul was set down, God had to find a new king. The prophet, Samuel, is instructed to go to a man's house named Jesse. He is told that once there, God would show him who the new king was. Samuel arrives at Jesse's house and says, "Get all your sons up here, line them up. The Holy Spirit is going to tell me who the next king is."

The sons begin to assemble, and in walks Eliab, tall and

handsome. Samuel thought to himself, "That's him. That's the guy." But God says to him, "That is not the guy." Why? Because God looks at the inward heart, but men look at the outward appearance.

This is a mistake we all make. I call it hijacked by talent, moved by flattery, or moved by appearance. We put people in places where they are not mature enough to be in that position. I think if you own any company or pastor a church, you have probably made that mistake, and you know what I'm talking about when I say hijacked by talent.

They're so good at what they do. I mean, I know there are some issues with their character, but I mean, how would I find anyone who can do what they do? They're talented. Does anyone understand what I'm talking about? You delay confronting them, and you walk on eggshells to keep them. You even raise their pay to appease them, but you already know they are not with you. You already know that if you had someone else just as talented, you would sit them down. But you don't, so you put up with it. You continue to compromise.

Dean Radtke said, "You would have a better worship service with only a juice harp and someone that knew they were not the best but truly wanted to worship and be part of your team, than with a team of worship leaders whose hearts were whacked out with pride." Dean told me, "Gary, you've got to clear the air. You've got to confront this situation and deal with it. You can't be insecure in leadership. You don't judge people by their talent or by their resume. You've got to get in there and do what God is telling you. I know he looks great, has awesome talent, but God is saying, 'That's not the guy.'" Here comes the devil's blackmail statement, "You do not have anyone to take their place!" But I know someone who does. God already knew of a young man who had His heart when God told Samuel to fire Saul. A young man who was a nobody, out tending sheep for his dad, his name was David, the next king of Israel.

When God spoke to me in Albania that I was to launch a TV ministry, that was something I had never thought of and never wanted to think of. I knew nothing about doing TV. But in Albania, God told me He was sending me to the nations, and TV was the means by which He was going to do it. But there were some major hurdles to overcome before that could happen. First, it would cost about $300,000 to get things started. Secondly, as I said, I did not know anything about doing TV. I had no equipment and no people on staff who knew anything about TV. The church was in the middle of building the Now Center Campus, and every cent was already allocated towards that project. There was no money. In my mind, it was an impossible mandate. I just could not see how it could happen. I wrestled with that decision for a month. I was miserable! Finally, I said, "Yes." I did not know how, but I said yes.

On a Sunday morning service, a man in my church, who came to my church about two years earlier, broke, walked up to me, and gave me $120,000 towards starting a TV program. I was totally shocked. Then, through some other events that God arranged, Drenda and I had the $300,000. Wow! Then an even more amazing event happened. Drenda was at a meeting, and a lady she did not know said to her, "If you guys ever do TV, call this guy." Drenda had not mentioned to her anything about doing TV; she had just met her. The lady wrote down the man's name and email address, and she stuck it in her purse.

A couple of weeks later, Drenda remembered the note she received from the lady and decided to email the man. He answered and said he would like to meet us. We made arrangements to meet, which we did, and we explained how God had spoken to us about doing TV. It was a great meeting, and we left him with some of our material, and he said that he would call us back. Eventually, he called us back and said that he would help us with our TV program. On top of that, he said that he would provide all the equipment as well as edit and produce the show. We were thrilled and set up a time to meet at our home to design a place in our home where we could tape the programs. That day arrived, and for the first time, he shared with us his history in producing TV. He told us how he was currently working with almost every major ministry on TV. I sat there stunned. I remember thinking, "How did this guy, someone with his experience, end up in my house, out in the country on my dirt road?" Only God could do that.

In another situation, Drenda was told through a dream to support a ministry couple that we had known for a while, and that we were to become a major supporter of what they were doing. Their ministry is known for sending teaching materials all over the world. Well, since God had spoken to me about going to the nations, that fit my passion perfectly. We loved supporting them and have been doing so for years. But one day, God spoke to me, saying that He wanted me to translate Drenda's and my

GOD KNOWS WHERE THE PEOPLE ARE. HE WILL BRING THEM, SO DON'T ALLOW YOURSELF TO BE HIJACKED BY SOMEONE'S TALENT OR CHARISMA.

Kingdom teachings and books into the world's languages and send them out. Well, I had been watching our friends do this for years. They have connections all over the world that can translate and print books and materials. When I told my friends about what God said to me, they offered their translation and printing team to help. Now we have translated our material into more than 50 different languages and counting, and have small groups in more than 60 nations worldwide. The point being that God knew what we were to occupy when He told us to support that couple. That one connection was the key that enabled us to occupy the territory God had for us.

God knows where the people are. He will bring them, so don't allow yourself to be hijacked by someone's talent or charisma. He knows where the Davids are, the graphics people you need are, or the IT person. He has been training them somewhere just for this moment, and He will speak to them!

Another tactic that Satan uses to gain access into your org chart and wreak havoc is through an offense. This is a big one in the church. The enemy can launch offenses everywhere, right? We read what Paul said about that church in Corinth, that there was jealousy and quarreling. He said they're babies.

Have you ever noticed how offended babies get? Wah. The baby picks up something you do not want them to have. No, no. Wah. They're getting all upset. "My toy, my toy!" Babies get offended so easily. They're going to get all upset because they didn't get to do this or that. You didn't give them the position or promotion they wanted, or you had to correct them. They will cry out, "That's not fair." You hear that a lot, "It's not fair." I think I have mentioned this before, but let's review:

NEVER PUT A BABY IN A PLACE OF AUTHORITY!

I'm not saying they can't grow up. I'm not trying to write people off. I want to write them in. But you will need to train and mentor these people, right? They all have giftings, and they all have assignments that God put in them to help you occupy the territory that God is calling you to occupy. As these offenses pop up, and they will, you will need to deal with them quickly before those involved go political with their offense and start recruiting people to their point of view. Soon, you will have a gang of people who have picked up the offense. Let's make one thing very clear. An offense stops the authority flowing down from the head quicker than a lightning bolt. You cannot let an offense fester. The Bible is clear on how to handle them.

If your brother or sister sins, go and point out their fault, just between the two of you. If they listen to you, you have won them over.

—Matthew 18:15 (NIV)

YOU CANNOT LET AN OFFENSE FESTER.

Go to that person. Don't go sideways. Don't gossip. Go to that person, right? If there is a problem that you can't handle, always go up with your comments, never sideways. In this type of situation, it is imperative that you keep the dialog and the comments in proper alignment with the org chart. I have found that most offenses are really just misunderstandings. Perceptions are sometimes greater than reality, and people like to read into a lot of things about situations that are not true. If you have to, get the two offended parties together and talk it out. Usually, that will work things out.

As a leader, you are responsible for communicating with your team, the boxes under you on the org chart. Good communication solves and prevents most of the problems people encounter, and will keep the authority and the power of God flowing. Your occupation of the territory God has entrusted to you will be successful, and you will find promotion in your future.

CHAPTER TWELVE

WARNING: NOT EVERYONE IS GOING TO CELEBRATE YOUR DESTINY

As we have discussed in this book, God has an awesome future for you, a destiny that is so great that it is far above what you even thought possible. But I want to make sure you understand that Satan hates God's plan for your life, and he will try to interrupt it from happening if he can. As I have said, God brings people around you, but you need to understand that Satan also brings people around you. You must be able to discern who is and who is not supposed to be on your team. You must watch out for the people who will try to persuade you away from your dream, away from your destiny. Sadly, there will be many people who are secretly hoping you fail. Your front-line team must be 100% for you and your vision. They must have already been proven in the fire of adversity and have proven loyalty to you. Why? Because you are going into battle together.

When you go to war against your enemies and see horses and chariots and an army greater than yours, do not be afraid of them, because the Lord your God, who brought you up out of Egypt, will be with you. When you are about to go into battle, the priest shall come forward and address the army. He shall say: "Hear, Israel: Today you are going into battle against your enemies. Do not be fainthearted or afraid; do not panic or be terrified by them. For the Lord your God is the one who goes with you to fight for you against your enemies to give you victory."

Then the officers shall add, "Is anyone afraid or faint-hearted? **Let him go home so that his fellow soldiers will not become disheartened too."**

—Deuteronomy 20:1–4, 8

Fear is contagious, but so is courage! Be sure your leaders are people of courage and stand with you and your vision. When Gideon was facing the army of the Midianites in Judges 7, he had 32,000 fighting men, but then God told him:

Now announce to the army, 'Anyone who trembles with fear may turn back and leave Mount Gilead.'" So twenty-two thousand men left, while ten thousand remained.

—Judges 7:3 (NIV)

More than sixty-six percent of his men left him! And actually, God whittled his fighting men down to only three hundred before the battle. And of course, you know the outcome; they completely won the victory. There is a very valuable lesson here. Don't be moved by the odds. If God is for you

FEAR IS CONTAGIOUS, BUT SO IS COURAGE!

and you hold fast to His Word and what He told you to do, you will see success.

I have had people on my team give commentary to other team members on why the plan I have just revealed will not work. If that is the case, send them home. You must have unity among your leaders, and they must believe that you have heard God, and that settles it. There is no room for debate.

There is a very sad story in 1 Samuel 23 that I want to bring to your attention.

> *While David was at Horesh in the Desert of Ziph, he learned that Saul had come out to take his life. And Saul's son Jonathan went to David at Horesh and helped him find strength in God. "Don't be afraid," he said. "My father Saul will not lay a hand on you. You will be king over Israel, **and I will be second to you. Even my father Saul knows this.**" The two of them made a covenant before the Lord. Then Jonathan went home, but David remained at Horesh.*
>
> —1 Samuel 23:15–18 (NIV)

Jonathan was a great warrior, and he and David were of the same spirit; they were best friends. In this passage, we can see that Jonathan already knows that David has been anointed by Samuel the prophet as the next king over Israel.

And he wants to be right beside David when David steps into this position. But David never saw Jonathan again!

> *Now the Philistines fought against Israel; the Israel-ites fled before them, and many fell dead on Mount Gilboa. The Philistines were in hot pursuit of Saul and his sons, and they **killed his sons Jonathan, Abinadab and Malki-Shua.***
>
> —1 Samuel 31:1–2 (NIV)

What happened? How could this happen? Wasn't Jonathan going to be second in command when David was placed as king over Israel? Yes, he was. So, what happened? Let me ask you a question first. Why did Jonathan go home? Why didn't he just stay with David and his six hundred men? He already knew that David was the new king, and his father was trying to kill him. Possibly, Jonathan wanted to stay involved to stay aware of what his father, Saul, was doing. Or Jonathan cared so much for the country that he wanted to stay involved to help protect his nation as he had done so many times in the past. The bottom line is that Jonathan allowed himself to be moved by familiar associations, obligations, and possibly intimidated by his controlling father. Jonathan should never have been on that mountain that day. King Saul was in rebellion. God could not bless him.

> *The Philistines assembled and came and set up camp at Shunem, while Saul gathered all Israel and set up camp at Gilboa. When Saul saw the Philistine army, he was afraid; terror filled his heart. He inquired of*

the Lord, but the Lord did not answer him by dreams or Urim or prophets. Saul then said to his attendants, **"Find me a woman who is a medium, so I may go and inquire of her."**

"There is one in Endor," they said.

So Saul disguised himself, putting on other clothes, and at night he and two men went to the woman. "Consult a spirit for me," he said, "and bring up for me the one I name."

But the woman said to him, "Surely you know what Saul has done. He has cut off the mediums and spiritists from the land. Why have you set a trap for my life to bring about my death?"

Saul swore to her by the Lord, "As surely as the Lord lives, you will not be punished for this."

Then the woman asked, "Whom shall I bring up for you?"

"Bring up Samuel," he said.

When the woman saw Samuel, she cried out at the top of her voice and said to Saul, "Why have you deceived me? You are Saul!"
The king said to her, "Don't be afraid. What do you see?"

The woman said, "I see a ghostly figure coming up out of the earth."

"What does he look like?" he asked.

"An old man wearing a robe is coming up," she said.

Then Saul knew it was Samuel, and he bowed down and prostrated himself with his face to the ground.

Samuel said to Saul, "Why have you disturbed me by bringing me up?"

"I am in great distress," Saul said. "The Philistines are fighting against me, and God has departed from me. He no longer answers me, either by prophets or by dreams. So I have called on you to tell me what to do."

*Samuel said, "Why do you consult me, **now that the Lord has departed from you and become your enemy?** The Lord has done what he predicted through me. **The Lord has torn the kingdom out of your hands and given it to one of your neighbors—to David.***

Because you did not obey the Lord or carry out his fierce wrath against the Amalekites, the Lord has done this to you today. The Lord will deliver both Is-

rael and you into the hands of the Philistines, and tomorrow you and your sons will be with me. The Lord will also give the army of Israel into the hands of the Philistines."

—1 Samuel 28:4–19 (NIV)

Certainly, Jonathan knew the state of his father spiritually and would know from his experiences with God that God would not be with them in battle. So why did he go? There are many possible answers, but I believe that his father was so controlling that even though Jonathan knew better, and he gave in to submitting to his father. It cost him his life.

DO NOT BOW TO OTHERS' OPINIONS, NO MATTER WHO THEY ARE.

You can win every battle the enemy brings against you as you contend for your destiny as long as you keep the enemy out of your camp. The fact is that some, if not many, of your people are hirelings, meaning they are just there for the paycheck. That is going to happen, and as long as you keep those people in the lower ranks of your team and you have good oversight and accountability over them, you will be alright. But your leadership team must walk in unity with you. Do not bow to others' opinions, no matter who they are. You need to hear God for yourself as the leader.

Watch out for familiar relationships, like family and friends, who mean well, but who are talking you out of what God says with subtle comments like, "Are you sure that is going to work? What makes you so sure? I wouldn't do that if I were you, you know that so and so tried that and it did not go well for them."

I know that you have respected these people in the past, and it is very easy for you to bow down to their advice; it is so familiar. But you must hold to what God says. Beware of friendships or other team members who may try to speak against you behind your back. Do not allow yourself to compromise what you know is right to protect a relationship. Do not allow your team to gossip or to hear gossip concerning what you are doing. I do not allow my team to post negative comments on Facebook or other social media sites concerning anything going on in our ministry or business. From time to time, be sure that you or one of your leaders reviews your team's social media accounts, just to see what you find there. You will be surprised!

REMEMBER, YOU CAN ONLY RECEIVE FROM THOSE YOU HONOR.

Do not allow your team relationships to become too familiar with your personal life. They do not need you as a close friend as much as they need you as a leader who hears

God. Remember, you can only receive from those you honor. When your team gets too familiar with you, and they see a weakness, as we all have them, they will find it harder to believe what you say.

Let me leave this chapter with this one piece of advice from the book of Nehemiah.

> *When word came to Sanballat, Tobiah, Geshem the Arab and the rest of our enemies that I had rebuilt the wall and not a gap was left in it—though up to that time I had not set the doors in the gates—Sanballat and Geshem sent me this message: "Come, let us meet together in one of the villages on the plain of Ono."*
>
> *But they were scheming to harm me; so I sent messengers to them with this reply: **"I am carrying on a great project and cannot go down. Why should the work stop while I leave it and go down to you?"***
>
> —Nehemiah 6:1–3 (NIV)

What a great answer! Remember it. You are doing a very great work as well, and you do not owe anyone your time that is not on board with your great assignment!

CHAPTER THIRTEEN

DESTINY IS WORTH IT!

When Joshua first came to the promised land, it was a land of conflict, full of dangerous enemies. Could this really be the promised land? Well, not in the state as he found it. But the Lord told him he was going to subdue it and bring it under God's dominion. I am sure that you have gone to a great resort, and they have pictures in the hall of the land before the resort was built, and it was just ugly land with nothing there that would lure you to stay. But someone did not see the land that way. Instead, they began to visualize what the land could be transformed into. They had a dream of it being so beautiful that people would come from all over the world just to enjoy being on that land. Yes, there is a fight for destiny, but you must remember one very important thing: God is with you, and He already has the plans to bring beauty to your future.

In all the stories I have covered in this book, I hope one thing sticks out to you: Stay faithful to God; He knows where you are at. Be loyal and trustworthy, even when it costs you something. Always be the answer and not the problem, even when it looks like there is nothing in it for you. God is watching, and He is your rewarder and your promoter. Yes, there will be times on the journey when it looks like you are making no progress. But let's remember Joseph, in an Egyptian prison with no way out, and in one day, he was brought out of that prison and set in place as the second in command of the nation of Egypt.

Your story is going to be a great story as well. Don't quit! There is a place called Destiny in front of you. God has ordained it. And when you get there and subdue it, it will be a thousand times better than you can even imagine.

—-Gary Keesee

ABOUT THE AUTHOR

Gary Keesee is a television host, author, international speaker, financial expert, successful entrepreneur, and pastor who has made it his mission to help people win in life, especially in the areas of faith, family, and finances.

After years of living in poverty, Gary and his wife, Drenda, discovered the principles of the Kingdom of God, and their lives were drastically changed. Together, under the direction of the Holy Spirit, they created several successful businesses and paid off all of their debt. Now, they spend their time declaring the Good News of the Kingdom of God around the world through Faith Life Now, their organization that exists to motivate, educate, and inspire people from all walks of life and backgrounds to pursue success, walk out their God-designed purposes, and leave positive spiritual and moral legacies for their families.

Faith Life Now produces two television programs—*Fixing the Money Thing* and *Drenda*—as well as practical resources, conferences, and speaking events around the world.

Gary is also the president and founder of Forward Financial Group and the founding pastor of Faith Life Church, which has campuses in Central Ohio.

Gary and Drenda, their five adult children and their spouses, and their grandchildren all reside in Central Ohio.

For additional resources by both Gary and Drenda, visit FaithLifeNow.com.

FINANCIAL REVOLUTION CONFERENCES

If you're a pastor or leader in your church, you probably have plenty of vision for your ministry. But do you have the money or resources you need to support the vision?

If your church is like most churches, the answer is probably *not quite* or even *no*.

Why?

We've found one of the biggest reasons is DEBT. So many Christians are being held *hostage* by debt.

Your people *WANT* to financially support the ministry and vision of your church, but many of them are living paycheck to paycheck with no hope of breaking free.

We can help.

For more than 25 years now, we've been working with churches of all sizes, helping them reach their goals and see their visions for their ministries become reality. And the best part is that this is completely free!

We help churches by helping their people. We can help *your church* by helping *your people*.

Learn more at **ftmtevent.com.**

YOUR FINANCIAL REVOLUTION 5-BOOK PAPERBACK BOXED SET

Scan to order your copy. →

Gary Keesee went from being completely desperate financially and physically to healthy and whole, paying cash for cars, building his home free from debt, starting multiple companies, and teaching hundreds of thousands of people about Kingdom living each week through television, ministry, and books just like these.

What changed for Gary, and how can it change YOUR LIFE?

Your answers are in the pages of THIS book series.

This isn't just another set of books with tips on how to fix your finances.

Full of fresh revelation, powerful examples from the Word of God, and inspiring personal stories about Gary and others who applied the foundational teachings from these five Kingdom principles in their own lives and experienced drastic change as a result, this series of books was written to help YOU experience real change in EVERY area of your life.

No matter your situation, there are answers. It's never too late.

You can have your own amazing story!

Join Gary Keesee on this incredible five-part journey of discovery that will completely revolutionize YOUR life… just like it did his.

This set contains paperback versions of Gary's complete *Your Financial Revolution* book series:

- *Your Financial Revolution: The Power of Allegiance*
- *Your Financial Revolution: The Power of Rest*
- *Your Financial Revolution: The Power of Strategy*
- *Your Financial Revolution: The Power of Provision*
- *Your Financial Revolution: The Power of Generosity*

Get your copy of the complete *Your Financial Revolution* five-book series at garykeesee.com.

You can also give at garykeesee.netviewshop.com/donate.

www.ingramcontent.com/pod-product-compliance
Lightning Source LLC
Chambersburg PA
CBHW071615030726
47598CB00001B/280